JUDITH VON HALLE, born in Berlin in 1972, attended school in Germany and the USA and subsequently studied architecture, graduating in 1998. She first encountered anthroposophy in 1997, and began working as a member of staff at Rudolf Steiner House in Berlin, where she also lectured from 2001. In addition she had her own architectural practice. In 2004 she received the stigmata, which transformed her life. Her first book was published in German in 2005, and she now works principally as a lecturer and author, having had a number of books published in German and English translation. She lives in Berlin with her husband.

By the same author:

*And If He Has Not Been Raised..., The Stations of
    Christ's Path to Spirit Man*
The Lord's Prayer, The Living Word of God
*Secrets of the Stations of the Cross, The Mystery of
    Transformation*

ILLNESS AND HEALING

and the Mystery Language of the Gospels

Judith von Halle

TEMPLE LODGE

Translated from German by Matthew Barton

Temple Lodge Publishing
Hillside House, The Square
Forest Row, RH18 5ES

www.templelodge.com

Published by Temple Lodge 2008

Originally published in German under the title *Von Krankheiten und Heilungen und von der Mysteriensprache in den Evangelien* by Verlag am Goetheanum, Dornach, 2007

© Verlag am Goetheanum, Dornach 2007
This translation © Temple Lodge Publishing 2008

The publishers acknowledge the generous sponsorship of the translation by Dr Carsten Bosse of Los Angeles, California

The author asserts her moral rights to be identified as the author of this work

All rights reserved. No part of this publication may be reproduced, stored in a retrieval system, or transmitted, in any form or by any means, electronic, mechanical, photocopying or otherwise, without the prior permission of the publishers

A catalogue record for this book is available from the British Library

ISBN 978 1 902636 98 6

Cover by Andrew Morgan Design featuring *Maestà: The Healing of the Blind Man* (1308-11) by Duccio di Buoninsegna
Typeset by DP Photosetting, Neath, West Glamorgan
Printed and bound by Cromwell Press Limited, Trowbridge, Wiltshire

Contents

Foreword ... 1

THE LANGUAGE OF THE MYSTERIES ... 9

Belief and clairvoyant research as foundation for understanding God the Son ... 25

The secrets of the language of the Gospels in their relationship to a new spirit knowledge ... 40

The hidden meaning of the Gospel words ... 43

    The temptation of Lucifer ... 43

    Christ and Barabbas ... 49

ILLNESS AND HEALING AT THE TIME OF CHRIST ... 53

Illnesses as karmic love-gift of the gods in the post-Christian era, and as influence of the adversarial powers in pre-Christian times ... 53

Changes in the aura of the human bodily sheaths ... 57

The nature of illness at the dawn of the new era ... 66

Faith and change of heart as precondition for healing at the time of Christ ... 70

Methods for treating illnesses ... 74

The occult background to 'gout'	74
The occult background to 'possession'	78
The healing of the man with dropsy	87
The healing of the woman with the issue of blood, and the raising of the daughter of Jairus	89
Christ's instructions to the healed	105
The healing of the servant of the centurion of Capernaum	116
The significance of the different locations of teaching and healing	121
The illness-inducing adversarial powers in their relationship with 'mountain' and 'water'	126
The healing of two possessed Gergesenes by the water	132
The ahrimanic underworld in the Jonah story	138
ILLNESSES TODAY	146
The nature of illnesses today	146
The causes of modern illnesses	156
The nature of 'non-karmic illnesses'	164
THE FUTURE IMPULSE OF HEALING	176
The Christian impulse of healing today and in the future	176

Approaches to Understanding the Christ Event

Volume 4

For Peter Heusser

I would like to thank the priest Veit Zschiesche and staff at The Christian Community in Karlsruhe, Germany, who in November 2006 kindly made it possible for me to give a lecture on the parables in the Gospels, which formed the basis for this book.

Foreword

This foreword aims to give some answers to questions I am repeatedly asked when I give lectures, or take part in discussion seminars.*

An unprepared reader might, quite understandably, be taken aback by the mode and content of some passages in this volume, since it includes descriptions of historical and supersensible facts and events which are related as self-evident truths without any reference to substantiating sources.

In actual personal encounter one can gain an authentic impression of the speaker, but in the inevitable absence of open-hearted personal contact with my reader — which makes it far easier to create a mood of human trust and dialogue as the basis for clear communication — I will try to record what I have to say in writing. I have formulated the following explana-

---

* While these questions have already been dealt with in the Introduction to the collection of lectures published under the title *And If He Has Not Been Raised...* (Temple Lodge Publishing 2007) not every reader will know this book, or recall the commentary there.

tions and answers very precisely, knowing that such clarity could be interpreted as lack of modesty. At the same time though – which is why I am willing to take this risk – such clarity alone makes it possible to give anything like a full answer to questions that people ask me.

The contents of this volume have arisen from my own spiritual experience, and do not represent any kind of hypothesis or speculation, except where I expressly say that I am unable to make any definitive statement about a particular event or set of circumstances.

However, not every description stems from the same source of experience and perception. My spiritual experience relates, on the one hand, to a direct – one could even say sensory – involvement in the historical events at the time of Christ. This experience, granted to me in 2004 after I received the stigmata, can be pictured as a kind of 'travelling back in time', involving all the sensory impressions we can have during ordinary waking life, but now in relation to a particular epoch and location. Thus the experience is not based on so-called visions or pure clairvoyance, nor imaginative pictures, but rather on direct witnessing of what

FOREWORD

actually happened on earth. Besides visual perceptions of the individuals participating in the events at the time of Christ, together with their surroundings, culture and way of life, all other senses available to us in normal waking consciousness are also involved. For instance the language being spoken can be heard, the ground beneath one's feet is felt, as are cold or heat.

The other source for the content presented here is quite different, yet no less authentic. It will be clear where accounts of the historical events pass over into a spiritual-scientific mode of observation. This may well appear more neutral and sober than descriptions of sensory experience at the time of Christ. This is no doubt right and proper from a certain perspective, since it involves as precise a 'translation' as possible of what is present and perceptible in the world of spirit. We can access intuitions of these cosmic facts when our ego or 'I', on passing beyond the threshold, separates entirely from the astral sphere so that we — or in other words our 'I' — enters the realm of objectivity. Everyone has impressions of this kind during sleep, yet we rarely succeed in carrying these back into waking consciousness. It is a difficult task and therefore one which involves great responsibility, to transform these objective facts which our 'I' has absorbed beyond the threshold into real knowledge that is as truthful as is ordinary sense perception on its own, self-apparent terms. We need to check repeatedly whether our spiritual perception truly corresponds to the conceptual framework to which we assign it. Only when all results stand up in the face of such scrutiny should the pupil of spiritual science feel entitled to pass on his findings as spiritual knowledge.

Many people have spiritual perceptions nowadays (one often hears that this faculty is on the increase) — for instance on the etheric or astral plane.

These perceptions remain useless however, or can often even trigger grave confusion, if their real nature and context remains hidden to those who have them. For instance, someone may have perceptions of the etheric world, immersing himself in the sphere of elemental nature beings. Yet statements about the elemental kingdom can only stand up to scrutiny, can only be truly objective, when we resurface again from that plane: in other words, when we do not solely immerse ourselves in the elemental beings' plane of experience but as it were raise it one level higher: to a perspective and point of observation from which we

FOREWORD

can not only report on the nature of the elemental word, but can also have knowledge *about* this world. It is like swimming in a great expanse of water, an experience which enables us to say that the water is deep and cold. But only when we emerge into the air again like a bird can we judge whether this stretch of water is actually a large lake or possibly an ocean; and whether and where the water is surrounded by land or not, and which continent it is on. So before we can authentically integrate our perceptions into a wider, overall context, they always need to be examined from a higher standpoint.

It is spiritual science's achievement that we are nowadays able to transform our perceptions, through clear, trained thinking, into knowledge that is faithful to truth and reality.

All the statements in this volume which do not contain sensory-based perceptions of events at the time of Christ derive from the source of knowledge just referred to. They are expressed cautiously, and with an appropriate sense of earnestness, and are in no way speculative interpretations. For this reason they may strike the reader as more factual or impersonal than the other accounts. This is due to the above-mentioned supra-personal level of objectivity beyond the threshold. Despite this they are my own authentic spiritual findings; and where, in contrast, they represent the findings of Rudolf Steiner, this is expressly stated.

This second type of spiritual perception is not in any way a consequence of stigmatization, since it was present before this occurred. Since then, though, it has intensified.

After my lectures were published in book form, some people asked me to give a precise exposition of my supposed path of schooling. I fully understand what underlies this desire, but apart from the fact that it was not my aim to address such issues in this book — since I do not wish to make my own destiny the main subject of my deliberations, but instead to use the resources available to render the Christ event more comprehensible — such a 'development manual' would be very short and probably not at all of the kind that people wish for or imagine. The mode of perception described above was already present in my early years, doubtless as a consequence of previous lives, and did not necessitate me pursuing, in this life, the arduous path of a hermit with all kinds of mortifications of the flesh and renunciations before my spiritual eyes were opened. Nor did it exclude, however, a certain discipline in my life as a consequence of self-evident engagement with spiritual realities. My discipline or spiritual reverence in this life can be seen as a consequence of preparation. Nevertheless, 'continuity of awareness' beyond the threshold is always only possible when, with the greatest engagement and commitment, one has absorbed and continues to absorb the Christ event; when, in a way that is devoted, loving, humble and grateful, one turns not only one's heart and soul but also one's powers of enquiry to the world of spirit — until one feels so strongly moved by that greatest of all events in humanity's evolution that one starts to feel a tangible sense of the stigmata. Then one can have the profound experience that the great sacrifice of the Redeemer was also accomplished for each one of us, for our own humble being — within which, however, lies the seed of the divine.

Thus my potential to live consciously into the spiritual cosmos — also described as continuity of awareness — was already present before stigmatization occurred. When I also started experiencing the historical events at first hand, rather than this remaining pure experience I was able to bring together my capacity for supersensible knowledge with the historical events I witnessed. You could say that the tool was already present before the material it was to work upon. If you want to construct a violin you need a good tool, ready to hand before you begin — rather than starting to make one at the same time as the instrument you're making. Without a tool you may have the finest wood as raw material, but you will be unable to make a violin with it. In the present case, supersensible power of knowledge can provide the necessary tool for investigating the spiritual background to sensory processes and historical events.

Berlin, March 2006 *Judith von Halle*

The Language of the Mysteries

The language of the Gospels conceals great riches in the form of profound insights into the evolution of the world and the human being. Yet these riches are not directly revealed to our modern understanding since the metaphorical language of the Gospels and the way it embodies meaning in sensory symbols — more or less irrespective of the particular translation or even of whether we possess an original manuscript — is no longer something we have easy access to. In the Gospels we find a powerful, dynamic pictorial language which, while conveying eternal content also still valid today, nevertheless derives from an era in which people still used this kind of pictorial language because their thinking had not yet entirely succumbed to intellectualism. With the advent of modern intellectual thinking however, understanding for this kind of language increasingly faded. The ordinary person of those days who heard Christ speaking in parables grasped it in what one might call a natural, self-evident way. For modern people, on the other hand, it represents a mystery whose deeper significance remains veiled as long as they regard the language of the Gospels as merely a poeticized variant of today's thought-permeated culture.

Anyone who studies the Gospels, in particular the Synoptic Gospels, will recognize that their whole underlying nature, along with the passages addressed to the non-initiated populace of those times, is today often considerably harder to decipher than those passages intended for the disciples close to Christ. The so-called interpretation of the laws, which Christ traditionally addressed to His disciples or the scribes or high priests, uses a language which seems closer to our modern way of thinking than that which reached the hearts of simple people of the time. We can seek the reason for this in the fact that Christ's speech heralded a future era — as did the Lord's Prayer also.* Despite their simple uneducated origins, the disciples had undergone a process of development through the schooling of heart and mind invoked in them by the Christ at work in their midst — as had also the high priests belonging to the priest caste, who had been

---

* See Judith von Halle: *The Lord's Prayer, The Living Word of God* (Temple Lodge Publishing 2007).

initiated over generations into the Mysteries of the Jewish people and the Messianic prophecy. Thus to these few people Christ was able to speak in a different, newer way — one which already required a certain ego or I strength in the recipient. Nowadays, when the age of the consciousness soul is well advanced, this capacity is no longer an expression of unusual development. This is why this type of speech seems more familiar to us, since it is closer to our contemporary mode of thinking than the pictorial and metaphorical language of pre-Christianity, which was spoken at the time of the Mystery of Golgotha and was most accessible to people then.

At the turning point of time 'I's, which had not yet developed to such a strong degree of consciousness as in our present times, were dwelling in increasingly degenerate bodies. Only through the sacrifice at Golgotha could these bodies be renewed and re-enlivened, thus creating the preconditions for the fourth member of the human constitution, the I, to awaken. At the time of Christ, souls still lived in a group-soul connection: their thinking flowed in the rhythm of long-gone times which, as Christ's appearance on earth drew near, was no longer adequate in a spiritual sense, but in fact rendered them deaf to the true inner content of spiritual revelations. Thus, at the time of Christ's arrival, a parable-like or pictorial language still 'housed' their understanding. Due to their spiritual degeneration, however, they nevertheless found it difficult to grasp the enduring and significant content with which Christ now filled this vessel of language.

In contrast to this prevailing mode, an ordinary everyday person would never have been able to understand what was meant if he had simply heard the following spoken with unvarnished directness: 'If you wish to gain knowledge of higher worlds, if you wish to understand the meaning of higher human soul development, and acquire this yourself, you will be unable to identify it by its outward magnificence and glory. It is not simply there as a given, and does not suddenly fill and permeate you during a single incarnation with the beauties of knowledge and wisdom. To gain it you must undergo an arduous path of schooling which requires your own strength of activity and will. Only by this means can you gain knowledge of higher worlds, and your achievement will be great and beautiful if, with patience and endurance, you nurture and cultivate deep in your inner life what at present appears insignificant, until it ripens into a beautiful stature of soul in which the divine hierarchies can find a dwelling.'

Such words would directly address human I forces, specifically indicating interconnections between the evolution of the world and human beings. A language of this kind can only be spoken and understood by people who have passed through 2000 years of post-Christian evolution of thought. At the time of Christ, in contrast, people would not have been ready to receive this more intellectual mode of language, and could not have grasped its meaning.

Instead, Christ gave the same teaching wrapped in the clothing of a parable:

> *The kingdom of heaven is like to a grain of mustard seed, which a man took, and sowed in his field: Which indeed is the least of all seeds: but when it is grown, it is the greatest among herbs, and becometh a tree, so that the birds of the air come and lodge in the branches thereof.* (Matthew 13, 31–32)

In ancient times the idea of a tree was connected with a whole sequence of images which passed through the human soul when someone heard the word 'tree'. Our modern thinking is abstract and rigidified, but can be enlivened and transformed by active engagement with Rudolf Steiner's science of the spirit. In general, however, we do not have a sense nowadays of what pre-Christian people experienced when they heard the word 'tree' — as an expression of the cycle of life and death, of the way the tree grows through the influx of the most varied cosmic and earthly influences, what we owe to its growth, how we can use it as a beneficent gift of the gods. Mostly, instead, we have the concept of an abstract, universal tree entity, composed of scanty or limited associations.

Some ethnic tribes, in contrast, still perform a 'tree initiation' to this day. The young novice is left alone by a tree in a deserted place for several days and nights, with the command to concentrate wholly on the inner and outer nature of the tree. Initial boredom is replaced by an unforgettable soul impression arising from the being of the tree, which gradually reveals itself in a huge multiplicity and diversity of life.

Likewise, when a person used to abstract, rational thinking today hears the phrase 'the birds of the air' he is likely to regard it as a romanticized pleonasm: birds

THE LANGUAGE OF THE MYSTERIES 15

are, after all, to be found in the air primarily, rather than on earth or under the water. For pre-Christian people however, a whole world would have opened up on hearing this, in relation to the kinds of bird which this phrase invokes.

At the dawn of the new era, people had this kind of pictorial understanding of language, even though this — now filled with the new Mystery revelations of Christ — could not lead them to direct understanding of Mystery content. Yet this was the sole means of speaking to them of these things.

Just as people before and during the time of Christ had a natural understanding of this metaphorical language of the Gospels, so today we have a natural predisposition to intellectual thinking. And just as the language in which we communicate content and concepts to each other, which is informed by our mode of thinking, would have been a Mystery language to people at the time of Christ, so today the language of those times has become a mystery to us.

Although conditions are changed, the ordinary person of today corresponds to the ordinary person of 2000 years ago in that he observes his world through the innate disposition with which birth endows him — and *only* in this way. Anyone who makes a serious attempt to deepen his understanding of world evolution, and who thus imagines himself into the stage of consciousness of the disciples, will be able to see the world through this mode of understanding. We place ourselves into this stage of perception, likewise, when we anticipate humanity's future general evolutionary condition and, without relinquishing the effects and achievements of intellectual thinking, create in ourselves a spiritually living conceptual world — as in the Goethean observations of nature which some have already embarked on.

In summary we can say that our logical mode of language and our intellectual thinking is to us today what parable and pictorial thinking were to the people of Christ's time. Those least practised in spiritual-scientific thinking will be least able to understand the ancient language of the Gospels, but will most easily grasp what Christ spoke to the disciples. In this they lag some way behind new developments in thinking — as did the ordinary people at the time, to whom Christ could not speak in the way He spoke to the disciples.

Our further spiritual development, therefore, requires us to fathom what is for us today the mystery of the pictorial language of Christ's time, by using the fruits of consciousness-penetrated thinking. By doing so we can participate in the revelations of the Gospels, and not simply stand there helplessly as the people once did in Palestine:

> *The same day went Jesus out of the house, and sat by the seaside.*
>
> *And great multitudes were gathered together unto him, so that he went into a ship, and sat; and the whole multitude stood on the shore. And he spake many things unto them in parables...* (Matthew 13, 1–3)
>
> *And the disciples came, and said unto him, Why speakest thou unto them in parables? He answered and said unto them, Because it is given unto you to know the mysteries of the kingdom of heaven, but to them it is not given... Therefore speak I to them in parables: because they seeing see not; and hearing they hear not, neither do they understand... But blessed are your eyes, for they see: and your ears, for they hear.* (Matthew 13, 10–16)

And then, after the parable of the mustard grain, Matthew adds:

> *All these things spake Jesus unto the multitude in parables; and without a parable spake he not unto them: That it might be fulfilled which was spoken by the prophet, saying, I will open my mouth in parables; I will utter things which have been kept secret from the foundation of the world.* (Matthew 13, 34–35)

But besides the parables themselves, the remarks or tales about the life of Christ which intersperse them also contain deeper truths beyond their apparent meaning, and these too cannot be understood without effort. Thus the following words do not merely describe outer circumstances: 'The same day went Jesus out of the house, and sat by the seaside. And great multitudes were gathered together unto him, so that he went into a ship, and sat; and the whole multitude stood on the shore.'

'Ordinary' people today, as characterized above, might well apply their innate, abstract thinking to conclude that Christ first sat by the shore, but that whenever larger multitudes gathered He boarded a boat and

THE LANGUAGE OF THE MYSTERIES 19

spoke to them from there, so that all would be able to hear Him.

But this was not the mode of thinking employed by the Evangelist Matthew. And those who understand that human thinking, and the language associated with it, has changed through the ages, will be able to see that these sentences embody far more than the — perhaps outwardly correct — idea presented by intellectual thinking. They may even find that these phrases contain a decisive pointer to a deeper understanding of the whole content of the passage. We can approach this by clarifying the way in which the words are arranged. Though few, they are all the more significant. Christ 'went out' of the house to 'sit' by the shore. (From an outer perspective, the Sea of Galilee is meant.) But why did He do this? Why did the Evangelist think it important to mention that Christ left the house and 'sat' by the shore? Why did he not simply write: 'Jesus spoke to the people in parables from the seashore'? And furthermore, why did He 'sit' in a ship and not stand up in it when He spoke to the multitude, whereas the people themselves 'stood' on the 'shore' — not boarding boats themselves — and did not sit down upon this shore while Jesus spoke to them?

Even such simple, apparently insignificant details can illumine a hidden treasure of knowledge, so that we may now start to conceive the profundity of the actual core messages embedded in and framed by these briefer descriptions.

Currently we are at a point in human evolution when it seems especially difficult to decipher the Mystery messages in the Gospels. The Word of God is, on the one hand, always living and can nourish us through *all* the ages with what we need in accordance with our times. Thus we can say that in every age the Gospels contained both a fundamental soul nourishment and also the greatest challenge to the human spirit. The Word of God adapts itself to humanity, as it were, in such a way that we can live and draw from it. On the other hand, the Gospels require new spiritual forces of us today, so that it seems as if we must adapt ourselves to and keep pace with them. This only *appears* to be the case, however, because people of past post-Christian eras regarded dedication to deciphering the secrets of the Holy Scripture as the highest fulfilment, whereas it can scarcely be seen as a highly prized aim of the modern materialistic age to devote oneself to occult research into the divine Word.

But it is precisely this which would be decisive for humanity's real progress. In an age, however, in which faith is increasingly derided as superstition, the prospects are poor that in the forseeable future the significance of Holy Scripture for the whole of humanity's evolution will be recognized.

Reverent and appropriate engagement with the content of the Gospels would have an enlivening repercussion on all areas of life, for the Gospels contain fundamental spiritual wisdom about world evolution — a wisdom which is revealed in Rudolf Steiner's anthroposophy, particularly his *Occult Science*. Over and above this, the Gospels can enlighten us about human evolution, right down to detailed and even medical aspects of the nature of the human being. The fact that Christ's appearance on earth is directly linked with the healing of humanity, and thus with medicine, is also confirmed by Rudolf Steiner's characterization of Christ as physician.*

---

* See Rudolf Steiner's lecture of 16 October 1918 in *How Do I Find the Christ?* (Rudolf Steiner Press 2006); also his lecture of 14 November 1909 in *Die tieferen Geheimnisse des Menschenwerdens im Lichte der Evangelien* (GA 117); and the lecture of 29 November 1921 in *Die Wirklichkeit der höheren Welten* (GA 79).

But the concept of medicine prevalent in the western world today scarcely corresponds, regrettably, to the art of healing invoked both in the Gospels and in anthroposophically extended medicine. The Gospels give us insight into a medicine which, under certain preconditions, leads to lasting healing — in other words is not limited to outer alleviation or elimination of symptoms, but addresses the very cause of an illness. If modern mainstream medicine* proposes that it too is capable of doing more than merely alleviating symptoms, and even demonstrates its successes in corresponding scientific studies, we have to remember that such successes are only medium-term or apparent ones. Real healing only occurs in the rarest instances, since orthodox medicine does not acknowledge the human being's connection as being of spirit with his body, nor the karma active in illnesses. Viewed from the perspective of spiritual science, therefore, real cures occur in mainstream medicine almost exclusively as a kind of by-product. If medicine fails to

---

* This is expressly not intended as a blanket judgement of all those who work and help within mainstream medicine. These remarks are focused, rather, on the view informing orthodox medicine that the causes of illness are found only at the physical, material level.

consider the curative effect of karmically-related illnesses on the human being's spiritual entelechy, instead of true healing it is much more likely to call forth new illnesses which may pursue us into our next or a subsequent life on earth. Karma must be fulfilled, and inadequate knowledge of the real circumstances can only hinder it by intervening improperly through treatment not specifically geared to the individual. In some circumstances, therefore, an orthodox medical intervention can actually lead to the opposite of the desired healing, by presenting an obstacle to karmic intentions.

The kind of medicine which is related in the Gospels, and to which in future we will surely have to find our way back, is an occult medicine that draws its forces from the realm of spirit. It is occult because the One who came to redeem humanity, to draw the germ of degeneration from our bodies and lead them to integrated healing, came to us from a kingdom that is not of this world, but from a world beyond, of which contemporary people cannot as yet develop full awareness. Those familiar with spiritual science are of course aware that this other world – the world of spirit

— penetrates our sense world and everything that lives within it. Thus it also works through us human beings. The human being is a being of spirit. He is a spirit, but one clothed in a fragile and corruptible vestment: he does not return to nothing when his physical vestment decays, but becomes once more a spirit amongst spirits. We call this vestment the human physical body. And thus every illness and every impetus for healing that is expressed through our body is connected with the human spirit.

But how do we reach a renewed understanding of medicine through the Gospels? The first step is to learn to read their language. Thus before we proceed to considering medical aspects in the Gospels — the healings performed by Christ — I want to touch on a few examples of how we can enlarge our understanding of language. Rudolf Steiner has already done this in relation to specific concepts such as the 'fig tree' or the 'ascent of the mountain'.*

---

* See Rudolf Steiner: *The Gospel of St. Mark* (Anthroposophic Press 1986), lecture of 22 September 1912.

THE LANGUAGE OF THE MYSTERIES 25

Belief and clairvoyant research as foundation for understanding God the Son

We can approach this Mystery language by two different paths, which are however successive rather than mutually exclusive.

A more or less fundamental basis for fruitful preoccupation with the texts of the Gospels is the insight developed by spiritual science that human concepts continually change over the centuries and millennia. Concepts, as we described above in relation to the word 'tree', alter according to the human being's stage of development and the cultural epoch in which he lives, and according to specific cultural contexts. Even the people of the Middle Ages and their language are already unfamiliar to us and hard for us to identify with. And much more distant still are the people of Christ's time and their life circumstances. How differently they perceived themselves and their surroundings, how different was their perception, their thinking, feeling and will.

For modern people, therefore, it is indispensable to read the Gospels with an awareness that they were composed at a time and in a cultural milieu when people thought, felt and expressed themselves differently, in a way which is no longer familiar to us. The period during which the language of the Gospels was spoken and taught is that of Christ's birth and death. The cultural context is in the broadest sense that of the ancient Hebrews, and it is into this that we need to transpose ourselves if we wish to comprehend the language of the Gospels, and the language used by Christ, or if we wish to gain insight into the healings initiated by Christ. Transposing ourselves like this is possible if we first acquire an awareness of the validity of spiritual science, by means of which we can release ourselves sufficiently from our modern patterns of thinking to open up to the authentic conditions and circumstances that flow to us from the past.

On 12 April 1914, Rudolf Steiner said:

> *... that we can find God the Father in philosophy; we cannot find Christ through any philosophy, by means of conceptual consideration. That is quite impossible... This is why we can never reach God the Son, the Christ, with the same kind of truth by which we reach God the Father. To reach Christ we need to add*

> *to philosophical truth the truth of belief or – since the era of faith is increasingly fading – the truth which comes from clairvoyant research...**

The secret of the Son, the 'idea' of the Son of God – in the Schillerian sense of a living, spiritual and creative idea – protects itself as it were through the conditions it invokes. Thus God the Son also remains in a certain sense inviolable through the fact that only those may penetrate to Him who free their hearts sufficiently to *believe;* or who sufficiently acknowledge the reality of the world of spirit that they work their way through to Him by means of the *knowledge of the spirit* – spiritual science – thus attaining insight into spiritual relationships and circumstances. The Son of God therefore remains hidden from all who rely on bare intellectualism or 'philosophy' alone, since such methods can know nothing of the *reality* of the Mystery of 'love or grace'.

Rudolf Steiner's statement touches on the two preconditions for understanding the Christ being: faith and/or supersensible knowledge.

---

* See Rudolf Steiner: *The Inner Nature of Man* (Rudolf Steiner Press 1994), lecture of 12 April 1914.

These are the two paths to God the Son. And they are the same paths, also, which we must pursue in order to immerse ourselves in the spirit and language of the Hebrew people at the time of Christ: a spirit which once imbued the authors of the Gospels, and in which their testimony is preserved for us.

There is however a certain distinction between coming to 'Christ, the Son of God' through faith, or, today, deciphering the Mystery language of the Gospels. Faith can open the gate of feeling insight for the truth of the Christ event, as this is described in the Gospels. It is a suitable means to lead us to God the Son. Behind this gateway opened to us by faith stand love and grace. We do not acquire a conceptual grasp of the content which clear thinking gives us through faith alone, but rather through what faith can open in us: through occult, 'clairvoyant research'.

Under no circumstances does the Word of the Gospels lose significance and effect if we do not study it by spiritual-scientific methods. The Gospels contain the Word of God, which is ever-present. But over time we acquire a different awareness of the nature and meaning of the Word. Nurturing a modern awareness of the meaning of the Word as such — the Logos — is the task to which anthroposophy has dedicated itself.

Today faith itself is not what leads us to an explanation of difficult occult Mysteries. It does however provide an almost indispensable foundation for deciphering these by means of spiritual science.

Since we no longer have atavistic capacities nowadays — which have been lost to make way for the development of the consciousness soul — the words of the Gospels do not conjure in us an immediate pictorial understanding of their hidden meaning. We can grasp their truth through faith, but not arrive by this means at a literal 'translation', an insight into their Mystery content, such as spiritual-scientific research can give.

Yet faith is the cornerstone of our understanding of Christ; and if in future it is to find itself confirmed and to a certain extent replaced by direct *knowledge* of God the Son, which will become possible through the development of new spiritual organs, it is nevertheless currently still of vital importance for ensuring that our relationship with the divine world is not lost during a period of inner upheaval in the human being.

It is therefore right to experience the current human condition as a real probation of the threshold. We are, after all, at a point where the pictorial consciousness of ancient times — that is, a naturally endowed understanding of the gods — is being lost, without as yet being fully replaced by the spiritual organs which the forces of our consciousness soul develop in us. It is these organs which could root us, with a new understanding of ourselves, in a knowledge of spiritual worlds. Since we cannot hearken back to the past, there is only one way forward if we are to avoid submerging our consciousness in the darkness of the perishable world of matter, and going under with it: to strengthen our faith and use the awakening powers of the I to pursue the arduous path of inner schooling which ultimately — to use the metaphor of Christ — will become a tree in which the birds of heaven nest.

At the dawn of the new era, faith was the only means of awakening to the being of Christ Jesus, and to become whole and healthy in body and soul. We can tell this especially from the fact that the disciples, whom we described as being exceptional for their time since they had already acquired a subtle, future-oriented, I-permeated consciousness and understanding of language, were only able to appropriate this in the presence of the thirteen. When He was amongst them and stood in their midst, the spirit-illuminating power of the Logos radiated over them, and He endowed them with what all human beings would only later be endowed with through the Resurrection. Through His immediate presence and proximity, it was 'given them to perceive the secrets of the kingdom of heaven'.

But when He was not with them, they did not have this capacity of knowledge, and were instead wholly dependent on their faith. And if this was not strong enough to replace the insights of direct perception, they grew weak, and were unable to perform healings as a matter of course or to remain fearless in their boat on the turbulent waters of the Sea of Galilee. Let us look for example at the Gospel of St Luke and the description of the storm at sea:

> *Now it came to pass on a certain day, that he went into a ship with his disciples: and he said unto them, Let us go over unto the other side of the lake. And they launched forth. But as they sailed he fell asleep: and there came down a storm of wind on the lake; and*

they were filled with water, and were in jeopardy. And they came to him, and awoke him, saying, Master, master, we perish. Then he arose, and rebuked the wind and the raging of the water: and they ceased, and there was a calm. And he said unto them, Where is your faith? And they being afraid wondered, saying one to another, What manner of man is this! for he commandeth even the winds and water, and they obey him. (Luke, 8, 22–25)

As we gain greater clarity about the foundations for a true understanding of Christ – faith or supersensible knowledge – an example of the language of the Gospels which appears to us to be metaphorical can show that insight into the supersensible realities underlying everything sensory can indeed reveal the spiritual background to this commentary. The description of the sea storm in the Synoptic Gospels can today be seen as a testimony to the struggle for autonomous individual consciousness in the disciples.

The water is calm when the Master boards the ship with them and the journey begins. But then He falls asleep and a mighty storm rises which buffets the ship so strongly that they are at risk of drowning.

The ship in which the disciples sit is their soul, within which they bear Christ Jesus. The power of I-consciousness boards their ship, thus entering their souls. The journey's destination is 'the other side', or the kingdom that is not of this world. But to grasp the 'secrets of the kingdom of heaven' which lie on the further side, the power of the I must be present, since the journey to the other world crosses a water which Rudolf Steiner once described as the 'sea of spirit being'.*

This journey goes smoothly until the power of consciousness of the Logos withdraws. The passage says He falls asleep. This means that the powers of His I are not available to the disciples for a while. It is not by chance that they are afloat on the waters of the lake and that these are suddenly lashed into a raging, foaming inferno. This is a trial for the disciples — one which aims to make them aware that on the waves of the 'sea of spirit-being' the human being must rely on his I. In fact, the soul can only experience this sea of spirit-being as smooth and transparent when — sus-

---

* See the Foundation Stone verse in: Rudolf Steiner, *The Christmas Conference for the Foundation of the General Anthroposophical Society* (Anthroposophic Press 1990).

tained by the impetus of I-consciousness — it can keep afloat upon it. If this power is lacking, the water appears, in contrast, as wild, deep and incomprehensible. The disciples are afraid they will go under in it, and the soul is at risk of being lost in its turbulence. Here the strength of the higher I has the function of the Guardian of the Threshold, which protects the soul from plunging into its own dark abyss.

Understandably, at the time of Christ the disciples were as yet unable to arrive at such a spiritual interpretation of their experience on the waters of the Sea of Galilee — which no doubt also occurred in sensory reality. We have already mentioned that people two thousand years ago did not possess today's mode of perception and knowledge. As though in a dream they absorbed the instructions and teachings of Christ, and we can see from this example how human consciousness has changed over the ages, how it has matured and how topically relevant today is what we can gain from a study of the Gospels. The disciples and their fate on the water become for us a living image of events in which we can experience our own inner struggles of soul and self-rediscovery.

In this way the secrets of the Gospels will gradually reveal themselves to us according to our stage of spiritual development, and in future times also will remain a precious store of insight which, with our present mode of knowledge, we cannot yet wholly fathom. And if one asks what occult secrets the circumstances of the stilling of the storm might still conceal — apart from the connection with the sea of spirit-being and evolution of the I — we can reflect that in future it may be possible for us to perceive why this metaphor of spiritual realities could also, simultaneously, have taken place on the physical plane; and how there is a purely scientific explanation for the fact that Christ Jesus was able to calm the elements.

But now let us look again at the importance of faith in the time of Christ. When the disciples awoke their sleeping Master, or in other words when their souls re-invoked the I of the Logos, without which they were at risk of going under, He said to them: 'Where is your faith?' (Luke 8, 25). Thus apart from His strength of consciousness which was directly available to them, there would have been another means to avoid the peril that threatened them: by having faith, or being able to have faith. Such faith is trust in the reality of the world of spirit and its power. We can assume that by drawing on such faith the storm of the 'sea of spirit-being' would not have arisen in the first place. In Matthew it even says: 'Why are ye fearful, O ye of little faith?' (Matthew 8, 26).

In the First Class of the School of Spiritual Science, the esoteric pupil is confronted with a test: that of facing his fear of creative spirit being so as not to fall into an inner abyss. One can find something similar in Rudolf Steiner's work *Knowledge of the Higher Worlds*. Without already having specific knowledge of higher worlds, the disciples' faith could lead them to the threshold of consciousness as long as this faith was strong enough to overcome their fear, their lack of trust in the spiritual power of the Creator over the earthly world.

At the transfiguration of the Lord on Mount Tabor, He was accompanied by three of His disciples, while the others remained on the plain and there met a man who asked that his lunatic boy be healed. When the Lord returned from the mountain, His disciples, the boy's father and a great gathering of people came to meet Him. When he saw Jesus, the man begged:

THE LANGUAGE OF THE MYSTERIES 37

> *Master, I beseech thee, look upon my son . . . ! And, lo, a spirit taketh him . . . and bruising him hardly departeth from him. And I besought thy disciples to cast him out; and they could not. And Jesus answering said, O faithless and perverse generation, how long shall I be with you, and suffer you? Bring thy son hither!* (Luke 9, 38–41)

This example also shows that either the presence of the Christ power was necessary for the disciples to carry out a healing, or that they should have had faith. Jesus's plaints about the disciples' lack of faith should be seen as a loving exhortation, with the aim of steeling and tempering their hearts. The formulation 'how long shall I be with you, and suffer you?' in contrast needs to be interpreted and transposed into our modern understanding as 'how long shall I be with you and *sustain* you?' In other words, how long will the disciples be dependent and reliant on Christ Jesus, on the presence and availability of His I? How long will His I continue to have to carry and sustain the disciples until they are, at least in faith, as strong as a rock so as to survive the time until their own I awakens?

How dependent the knowledge of Peter is on the Son

of the living God, that is, on the living I AM, is clear not just from the fact that this moment of insight is assigned a whole chapter in the Gospels, but also from the reaction of the disciples after the storm at sea has been calmed: 'And they being afraid wondered, saying one to another, What manner of man is this! for he commandeth even the winds and water, and they obey him.' 'Who is this?' they ask. In other words, they do not yet know their own I. Just as, today, an infant does not yet have a direct awareness of his I but is still dependent on his mother's configuring I-forces, the I of Christ which entered them was in a certain sense still unknown to them. Their own I was however still more unknown. Herein also lies the special quality of the Whitsun event for the disciples. Unlike the rest of humanity they were able to grasp their I more quickly at the first Whitsun since they had been prepared for a life with the awoken fourth member of their being — because Christ Jesus had lent His own I during the time He dwelt amongst them. Thus at the dawn of the new era, faith was indispensable for a living connection with the world of spirit, since people's ancient vision of the gods was no longer available to them. It had faded in preparation for the moment when, for the first time in human evolu-

THE LANGUAGE OF THE MYSTERIES

tion, the transition from 'faith' to 'supersensible perception' would be brought about through the human being himself. This transitional moment arrived on Easter Monday when the Risen One appeared to the eyes of Mary Magdalene. She believes He is the gardener, until He addresses her with the word 'Mary!' (John 20, 16). She falls to His feet and wishes to touch Him since she believes this is the re-awoken Jesus of Nazareth in His old body. But He gestures her away with the words 'Touch me not! For I am not yet ascended to my Father...' (John 20, 17). Only then does she awaken to the recognition that she beholds God the Son, clothed in a transformed body; only then does she perceive the Risen One as resurrected. Already before this encounter she had run to the disciples who did not wish to believe that the corpse of the Lord had vanished. John and Simon Peter were the only ones who went to the grave and there saw the linen cloths cast aside in which the body of the Crucified Lord had previously been wrapped. Here the Gospels say: 'Then went in also that other disciple, which came first to the sepulchre [Peter] and he saw, and believed. For as yet they knew not the scripture, that he must rise again from the dead' (John 20, 8–9).

The scripture is fulfilled when they also encounter the Risen One. They recognize Him and perceive that the prophecies of the prophets and their master are true. This is the historic moment of transition from faith in the spiritual world to supersensible perception of it. Apart from John, only Paul bears his own unique form of testimony to perception of the reality of the secret of the Risen One.

Since those days humanity has developed towards supersensible perception of God the Son, as is cultivated in true Rosicrucianism and anthroposophy.

Where knowledge is not yet fully present, faith continues to form the foundation of religious life.

The secrets of the language of the Gospels in their relationship to a new spirit knowledge

Now let us turn to an exploration of the secrets of the language of the Gospels. Here, alongside faith, we will need perceptive insight into, on the one hand, the pictorial, ancient Hebrew mode of language and, on the other, the occult treasures of knowledge which Christ gave us in His words and deeds. That this is unquestionably no easy task was already suggested when we spoke of the threshold situation in which we currently find ourselves, since ancient clairvoyant perception has now wholly faded and we therefore have no innate understanding of the metaphorical language used at the time of Christ. Nor have we mostly as yet been able to develop spiritual organs on the spiritual-scientific path of schooling to an extent that would enable us, with utmost certainty and without doubt or fear, to pursue our own spiritual research. The human consciousness soul, still in its infancy, is here put to a hard and often impossible test by the ever more prevalent world view which renders everything materialistic.

Thus we stand at the gateway to a new state of consciousness. If we look back, we see only darkness; and when we look forwards, likewise, the path at first seems shrouded in gloom. Precisely for this reason a loving, spirit-imbued study of the Gospels is so precious today, for the language we encounter in them not only conveys the truth of the divine world of spirit but also directly embodies it, and we come into contact with this world if such language becomes our inward experience. For every person, therefore, reading these texts today gives a spirit-configuring strength, and acts as balm to the soul.

The future-oriented nature of the language of the Gospels is apparent in the great challenge which it represents for our occult research. Likewise, the disciples themselves did not have self-evident understanding of the parables. They lacked the ancient pictorial understanding more than the ordinary folk who were unable to replace it with perceptive awareness of the Christ spirit – which, in the midst of the twelve, was able to ensure understanding of 'the secrets of the kingdom of heaven'. The disciples were in a situation similar to our own: through the representative presence of Christ they could experience an awakened I consciousness as long as He was amongst them. Yet since this was not their own I, grown in strength through several post-Christian incarnations, they did not yet possess the organs of spirit necessary to grasp occult secrets concealed in the metaphorical language and parables of the Lord.

The Synoptic Evangelists largely keep to this metaphorical language which has become a mystery to us, whereas John, endowed with the higher members of the Baptist given to him from the world of spirit at the raising of Lazarus,* uses a language which, according to Rudolf Steiner, must be taken literally.

For this reason, in relation to the pictorial and metaphorical language of the Gospels, our main focus will be on the Synoptic Scriptures.

The hidden meaning of the Gospel words

The temptation of Lucifer

We still stand before the gateway of knowledge, and therefore all the words of the Gospels can appear to us as parables.

One of the many examples of the language of the Gospels which is not explicitly 'designated' a parable, but which shows nevertheless how necessary it is to re-enliven ancient Hebrew concepts through spiritual science if we are to understand them today — and thus penetrate to insight into Christian teachings — can be found in Christ Jesus's temptation by Lucifer.

---

*See Rudolf Steiner's last address dated 28 September 1924 in: *Karmic Relationships*, Vol. IV (Rudolf Steiner Press 1997), and the notes to this by Marie Steiner in the German edition (GA 238).

> *Then the devil taketh him up into the holy city, and setteth him on a pinnacle of the temple, And saith unto him, If thou be the Son of God, cast thyself down: for it is written, He shall give his angels charge concerning thee: and in their hands they shall bear thee up, lest at any time thou dash thy foot against a stone. Jesus said unto him, It is written again, Thou shalt not tempt the Lord thy God.* (Matthew 4, 5-7)

Let us now try to fathom these words through spiritual science with the powers of consciousness available to us, and with our knowledge of world evolution and its connection with the adversary forces.

Lucifer urges the Son of God to climb upon the pinnacle of the temple. We can imagine this picture: the Son of God is led into the temple area and ascends to the highest elevation of the temple building. From here He is urged to cast Himself down. But naturally this picture contains a deeper significance.

Firstly, this isn't just any building but the temple of God, the most sacred place for the Jewish people since they settled in Israel and Hiram Abiff built the first temple under King Solomon's command. For initiates, the temple was the microcosmic reflection of the macrocosm, into which the Logos was one day to be led. Within its interior the initiation pupil would be placed into the so-called temple sleep so as to raise his soul to the spirit of Christ, whose entry in future times into the physical body could thus be perceived. After this initiation, the pupil found inner certainty that he would one day encounter the Son of God with all his senses in a human body, whereas as yet he could only see Him supersensibly by roundabout means when his soul departed from his body during the temple sleep.

In the pre-Christian Mysteries, one had to strive towards God the Son, whereas in future times the human being would become able to find Him within his own earthly body, as God Himself moved towards human earthly beings. Thus Jewish initiates regarded the temple as symbol of the physical body healed and sanctified by God the Son, and only in such a body could the human being turn his face and perceiving heart to the glory of God the Father. For this to happen, however, the Son must descend from divine heights in order to renew and heal the body. And this could only happen through a divine sacrifice which revealed the secret of the Son, that of selfless love. The forces of decadence to which earthly human beings had become subject through the influences of Lucifer and Ahriman could only be overcome if the spiritual sun illuminated the realm of darkness by entering the shadow kingdom of the adversary powers and, through this greatest imaginable sacrifice, transformed the death of matter into life of the spirit.

The ancient Hebrew people had the mission of creating the conditions necessary for the incarnation of the Logos, and in this sense the temple in the Holy City was a promise in stone of the forthcoming influx of divine sun forces into the earthly body. Only then — through the Son's sacrifice — would the earth reveal the Father's Creation in perfected form.

Now Lucifer demands that Jesus of Nazareth should stand on the pinnacle of this same temple, the reflection of the divine kingdom of God. He should elevate himself *over* the Creation of the Father before the sacrifice has been performed. By this means Lucifer aims to render impossible the path human beings can take in future through the Christ sacrifice: the path through the Son to the Father. In the Jewish Tree of Sephiroth, the upper triangle, consisting of the 'chockmah', 'binah' and 'keter' sephiroth, forms a roof

THE LANGUAGE OF THE MYSTERIES

over the middle and lower human organization. At the pinnacle of this roof, over 'keter' or the 'crown' — that is, over God the Father — Christ Jesus is urged to stand, denying the Trinity by drawing love, the heart forces that should kindle the middle realm of the human organization, up into the heights, and placing it over the forces of the head.

And then Lucifer uses an excerpt from the Psalms to tempt Christ Jesus and induce Him to invoke the help of the Father as He falls into the depths: 'For he shall give his angels charge over thee, to keep thee in all thy ways. They shall bear thee up in their hands, lest thou dash thy foot against a stone' (Psalms 91, 11-12).

Wholly devoid of its actual meaning and context, the tempter quotes this passage from holy scripture. In this Psalm, in fact, what is said is that God proves his faithfulness to the one who trusts in him alone. Right at the beginning, as if from the mouth of a faithful person, it says: 'My refuge and my fortress: my God; in him will I trust' (Psalms 91, 2). And at the end, as if from God's mouth: 'Because he hath set his love upon me, therefore will I deliver him: I will set him on high, because he hath known my name' (Psalms 91, 14). Thus the precondition for the protection which God grants human beings is their commitment to one God, the Father.

As the second luciferic temptation also shows, in which Christ is shown the land of Israel from the top of a mountain, and this is promised to Him as His kingdom — a kingdom of *this* world — if He will cast himself down before the tempter and worship him, the issue at stake is worship of the one God. Thus, to the tempter's promptings to cast Himself down from the pinnacle of the temple, Christ Jesus significantly answers with a Mosaic phrase which the representative of divine wisdom once spoke: 'Thou shalt not tempt the Lord thy God' (Matthew 4, 7).

These words were once addressed by Moses to the people after he received the Ten Commandments and warned them against the worship of many gods, or idolatry. Thus it says: 'Hear, O Israel: The LORD our God is one LORD: And thou shalt love the LORD thy God with all thine heart, and with all thy soul, and with all thy might... Ye shall not go after other gods... Ye shall not tempt the LORD your God' (Deuteronomy 6, 4-5; 14; 16).

This is how we should understand the temptation. Christ Jesus is being asked to elevate Himself above the highest level of the world of the hierarchies without having passed through the bitter valley of sacrifice. Lucifer wishes to bring Him under his sway by promising Him things He could attain prematurely, without avowal of God the Father, and without the sacrifice performed in devotion and love.

Christ and Barabbas

Another brief example of the concealed meaning of the Gospel words can be found shortly before Christ is condemned on the morning of the first Good Friday. This is the moment when Pilate offers the people one last opportunity to save Jesus of Nazareth from death. Pilate is standing on the broad exterior steps of his palace, facing the judgement square. At the foot of the steps stand Jesus of Nazareth to his right, and to his left Barabbas, the criminal. We can recall this moment through the words of the Matthew Gospel:

> *Now at that feast the governor was wont to release unto the people a prisoner, whom they would. And*

they had then a notable prisoner, called Barabbas. Therefore when they were gathered together, Pilate said unto them, Whom will ye that I release unto you? Barabbas, or Jesus which is called Christ?... They said, Barabbas. Pilate saith unto them, What shall I do then with Jesus which is called Christ? They all say unto him, Let him be crucified... Then released he Barabbas unto them: and when he had scourged Jesus, he delivered him to be crucified. (Matthew 27, 15–17; 22; 26)

Here the play of words between the name 'Barabbas' and the phrase 'Jesus which is called Christ' is the key to a deeper understanding of this metaphorical language and the occurrences it describes. The passage does not merely indicate the obduracy of the people of Israel who do not acknowledge their Saviour, but it also vividly conjures the working of higher spiritual powers and the way these bring about the destined and divine plan to save humanity.

On one side of Pilate stands the One *which is called Christ* – a name accentuated twice in the Gospel. There stands Christ, the Son of God. On the other side stands the criminal Barabbas. The Hebrew name for the

THE LANGUAGE OF THE MYSTERIES 51

Greek form of Barabbas is 'Barabba' or 'Bar Abba'. Translated this name means 'God's son'.

Thus two sons of God stand opposite each other: an inviolate one and a sinner. And the decision must now be made between them. Barabbas, the impure son of God, represents sinning humanity. He is a sinner who stands for transgressing mankind which has fallen under the sway of the luciferic and ahrimanic adversaries. And naturally he is released. His release however is not brought about solely by the fact that Pilate pardons him, for we know that Pilate would have had no power if this were not given him from above (cf. John 19, 11). Barabbas cannot be given over for crucifixion at this point since there would be no sense in bringing death to the transgressive representative of humanity. Humanity would then be led into the realm of Ahriman, and in death would never have come to eternal life. The sinless Representative of Humanity must meet death instead – the one who bore the body of the Nathan Jesus, which from the beginning of the world was preserved in the heavenly realms from sullying by the adversary forces. Thus God sent his once born Son to redeem humanity – to redeem Bar Abba. Only in this way is Bar Abba truly released.

Following these examples of the metaphorical Mystery language of the Gospels, the stories described in them of illness, and healing through Christ, can now be examined more closely.

Illness and Healing at the Time of Christ

Illnesses as karmic love-gift of the gods in the post-Christian era, and as influence of the adversarial powers in pre-Christian times

A more careful study of illnesses at the time of Christ, as these are mentioned in the Gospels, in some cases in great detail, shows that disease at the time of the Mystery of Golgotha was different from today. Some of the illnesses described are entirely unknown to us, and if we think we might nevertheless identify them as diseases still known today, we can be certain that they are almost exclusively ones which are rare today and of marginal significance.

We can seek the reason for this in the fact that the members of our being are today differently constituted and organized than was the case in pre-Christian times. The development of the consciousness soul today enables us to form a perceptive awareness of the reality of karma and its significance for both our soul-spiritual and physical development. Only through the

Mystery of Golgotha and germinal development of the fourth member of our being, could karma arise as we know it now. The I, which awoke in us through the sacrifice of Christ, now continually and necessarily conflicts with the lower bodily sheaths of our being, so as to purify and gradually spiritualize them. The advances, but naturally also the errors we make in this process, affect our destiny in future lives on earth. These effects include illnesses — or, more precisely, karmic illnesses. Thus karmic illnesses should not be viewed as scourges and punishments from the gods, but as an aid to our further development lovingly created by the gods, so as to help bring back into equilibrium what has arisen through all too mistaken thinking, feeling or deeds. The karmic illness that arises in a current life is nowadays often the last opportunity to compensate for imbalances created in a previous life.

Before the Mystery of Golgotha, divine beings had a different connection with the human being's illnesses. The influence of the fallen spirits Lucifer and Ahriman was, one can say, tolerated to some extent by the divine Trinity until the former had brought the human being to a certain stage of self-awareness – which would however have led to irreversible decadence without the Son God's deed of redemption. Up to that radical turning point in human evolution introduced by the incarnation of Christ, the dark spirits therefore intervened directly in human life, causing illnesses to arise.

The Logos, who at this point had not yet united with the earthly destiny and karma of the human race, and still dwelt in cosmic heights, only indirectly intervened in this process. The basic nature of this mediated intervention was God's non-intervention, in so far as illness caused by the demons manifested directly in a person's current life and not in a subsequent one. An I that had not yet awoken to awareness of the idea of karma could not yet have established a connection between immoral conduct in one life and the outbreak of an illness in another. By allowing the ravages of the demons to take their course in the human being's physical, etheric or astral bodies, as immediate consequence of his transgressions, the good God could nevertheless make illness a means to the good, that is, to a change of heart in the sick person. Illness had an almost pictorially tangible effect on a person, who in this way was able to develop a connection with his own pre-illness conduct. We will see, however, that such inner change occurring through a destined illness did not yet have the intrinsic power at the time of Christ to lead to a healing of the physical organism. This is also why the people regarded Christ as — if not the Messiah — at least a great prophet and healer. It was He who could heal people of their physical illnesses, which is why He very quickly became known throughout the country, and thousands made pilgrimages to Him in the hope of finding help. It was here that the Christian element entered the human being. The I forces of the Christ triggered a spontaneous process of healing.

Before the Mystery of Golgotha, people experienced their illnesses as a punishment from God for their sinful way of life. By this time, a naturally endowed vision of and contact with the divine world had long faded, together with a sense of its true connection with human destiny. This is why the priests themselves scarcely knew that it was not God who sent a demon to plague human beings with illness, but that, before the appearance of Christ, this God could not really intervene in an outbreak of disease because of his 'pact' with the adversarial forces.

In summary we can say that an illness today is usually a gift of the good gods whereas *before* the Mystery of Golgotha it manifested outwardly through the influx of spiritual adversaries. In those times, it can be said, illnesses were also in a certain way karmic in the higher sense that the effect of Lucifer and Ahriman on humanity was tolerated; but the karma of illness did not pass on from one incarnation to the next.

Changes in the aura of the human bodily sheaths

At the dawn of the new era, an outwardly manifesting illness was in most cases caused by a disturbance and disorder of the astral body. In other words, illnesses were luciferic in origin. In contrast to today, ahrimanic illnesses were not nearly so common, since the dominion of Ahriman prior to the Mystery of Golgotha was primarily confined to the realm beyond the threshold. Ahriman was the regent of the realm of death, of hell or Hades, and played a decisive role in the human being's destiny after death. It was Ahriman's intention to bind the human being entirely to the earth's dying forces at that precise moment when he must release his spiritual being from its anchorage in the earth's interior. Lucifer, in contrast, had been working directly upon earthly life since the Fall, affecting the human being's increasingly dominant astral body. This threatened to overburgeon and stifle the unprotected seed of the I which the Elohim had implanted in the inner human being in earliest times.

How did it specifically happen, however, that in ancient times the luciferic forces in the human being's astral body could grow to such effectiveness? The human being and his bodily sheaths were then quite differently constituted from today. In speaking of these ancient times I am referring here to human evolution during the first, second, and also third post-Atlantean cultural epoch, during which the human being's earthly, physical existence was connected in a quite different way with the astral: it was spread out across the starry heavens. If one wished to depict the astral and auric nature of a human being of the first post-Atlantean epoch, it would appear very different from the way it is perceived by spiritual vision today. One would in fact certainly not have found it in direct proximity to his physical body, but, at the time of the ancient Mysteries, it dwelt in the planetary spheres, in the realms of the gods.

In the very earliest times, likewise, scarcely any egotistic element was present in the human being, for his astral element lived not, in the first place, in individualized form, but in a group-soul context.

To sketch this condition schematically, we would have to depict the human being in his physical body and over him the planets. At that time he could suck in his astral nourishment from these planetary spheres, since his astral element was spread across the heavens, and connected with his earthly being only by something like a silken thread: this connection was very 'thin', streaming outwards into the planetary spaces, to the gods' realms of activity, and back again into his earthly being. The earthly human being received his impulses as though in sleep, through his astral element emanating from the dwellings of the gods. In other words he awoke outside his body in planetary space, and in his body his consciousness slept.

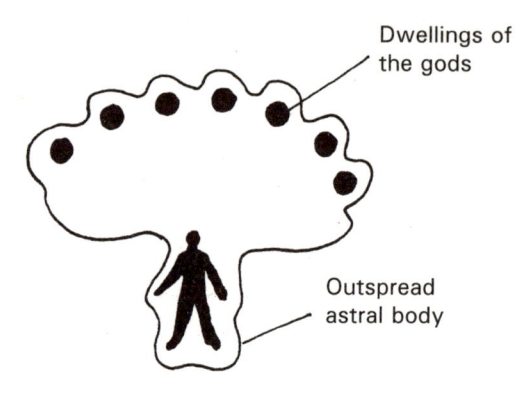

[Figure: Dwellings of the gods (dots around a cloud shape); Outspread astral body (human figure below)]

Fig. 1

In the age of the Greeks, which falls in the fourth post-Atlantean epoch, one sees how human soul qualities are still ascribed to the gods and vice versa. The Egyptian gods, likewise, reflect nothing other than astral nuances of the human being, who was of course directly connected with them. Thus the human constitution of bodily sheaths appeared very different from today, and altered over the course of time. The more that human beings came into contact with matter, and the more this played a part in their earthly existence — beginning roughly with the ancient Persian epoch — the more their relationship with planetary space also altered. Initially people saw the godhead outside of their own surroundings, but then increasingly within the closer periphery of the self; and by the time of Christ people felt this self to be wholly contracted. This led to people having a different perception of themselves. Whereas in ancient times a person had relatively few egotistic drives, since he was spread out across astral space with other human souls, in later times – towards the Mystery of Golgotha – his soul nature increasingly contracted. He drew it ever closer to himself, at the same time sundering himself from astral space.

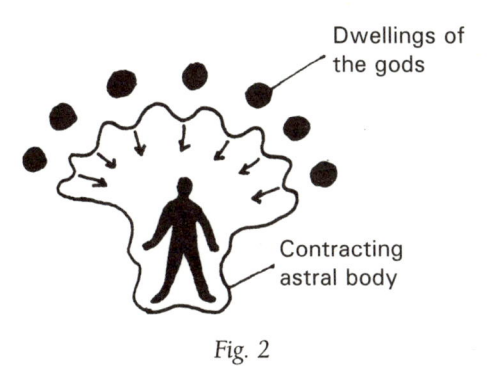

Fig. 2

The more this sundering process occurred, the stronger was people's perception of their own being in differentiation from their surroundings and other people. This development also inevitably led increasingly to egotism since the powers of the I had not yet awoken. People lost an atavistic awareness of what the good gods were, confusing these good gods whom they believed they had taken with them in their astral body, with the impulses of quite different spirits.

Amongst the Jewish people this path into egotism unfolded in the most 'healthy' way — to use an apparently absurd formulation to clarify this process. I mean by this that the Jews, who in this context may be called the 'chosen' race, were the only people of that time able to manage the contraction of astral bodies in a healthy way, since all their expectations were focused on the arrival of the Messiah, and thus their gaze was turned towards planetary forces. In the future these forces were to unite with the earth in such a way that they would one day be found wholly within the earthly human being. Under the guidance and leadership of its high initiates, the Jewish people were expecting a cosmic power to descend to the physical plane and come into close proximity with the human individuality, and in fact directly enter it. It is true that the Jewish people only received this direct connection with the Logos through the Mystery of Golgotha, so that their rituals and acts of worship at the time of Christ were also no longer filled with spiritual life, but nevertheless they did prepare themselves in a unique way for the appearance of the Logos in earthly existence. Those cultures which did not make themselves into vessels to receive the descent of God the Son and instead, despite the loss of their astral bodies' connection with the cosmic plane, pursued their old rites and traditions, irreversibly lost their contact with the gods. The 'heathen' gods — in whose midst people in ancient times had lived in their astral aspect spread wide in the cosmos — could no longer make themselves known from their planetary dwellings to human beings' contracted and even sundered astral nature. This could only be given through Christ, the sole representative of the divine hierarchies to descend into a physical human body, thus bringing down into human beings a knowledge of the divine cosmos. The other gods remained in the heavenly kingdoms however, and the people of Christ's time, in the altered constitution of their bodily sheaths, no longer found contact with them, which is why their rites became hollow and inevitably degenerated into heathen and demonic practices.

The sketch below aims to give a picture of the astral nature of the human being at the dawn of the new era, as this appears to occult vision:

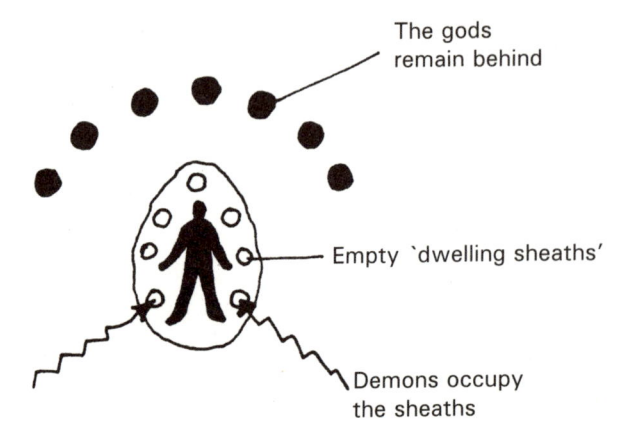

Figure: An astral egg containing a human figure with empty "dwelling sheaths" (small circles) inside; above, a semicircle of dark dots labeled "The gods remain behind"; below, wavy arrows entering the egg labeled "Demons occupy the sheaths".

Fig. 3

Thus the human being is no longer connected with the cosmos through his astral nature as he was in ancient times. Instead the latter has incorporated itself around him, as we know from Rudolf Steiner's descriptions of the human being today. As schematic indication the astral body is here depicted as a kind of egg permeating the human being, in which he stands and which envelops him. But this astral egg now appears strangely different to the way in which we are nowadays used to thinking of it. The astral body had gradually and increasingly contracted around the human being's etheric and physical bodies, and at the point of its 'sundering', the human being had taken into his astral body the empty sheaths of the planetary places of the gods. The gods' dwelling places, which were previously also the place where human astral bodies resided, stand bereft of them in the firmament at the dawn of the new era, and only the gods remain behind there. The gods' dwelling places were therefore still inhabited by the gods, but were orphaned or bereft of human astral bodies. These bodies had however brought with them the empty sheaths of those cosmic places in which they had once dwelt and from which they had drawn living nourishment, but it was not possible to bring the gods themselves as well. If one could have observed this process of astral evolution at the time, with the eyes of spirit, one would have seen how the empty sheaths of the gods' dwellings were brought down into human astral bodies, and how these empty sheaths, without their divine inhabitants, ultimately formed something like holes in human astral bodies (see Fig. 3 on page 64).

And now it was inevitable that something would

wish to incorporate itself into these uninhabited sheaths within human astral bodies: something whose dwelling was doubtless in the spiritual spheres and was not human, but had fallen, and fallen out of the advancing evolution of the hierarchies who inhabit the planetary spheres. Into the empty sheaths of those places of the gods there entered the spirits which the Gospel refers to as demons. Hosts of luciferic beings now populated human astral bodies, making their mischief there. This process, which culminated shortly before the Mystery of Golgotha, was in a certain sense unavoidable, since the human I had not yet fully awoken. Thus the human being stood there without guidance. Neither the I AM could take hold in him to create order nor — as in the ancient times of the Mysteries — could the divine hierarchies work indirectly on his earthly nature from their dwelling places.

The nature of illness at the dawn of the new era

The origin and cause of illnesses at the time of Christ, and the way in which Christ Jesus healed people, are different in several respects from processes of illness and healing today. Only relatively few people could receive healing from Christ at that time, although He healed around eighty to a hundred people a day on some days of His earthly existence. Blind, lame and deaf people came, and we read of people with gout, dropsy or those who were possessed by demons. Many of these illnesses were caused by a particularly strong luciferic occupation of the empty capsules from the gods' dwelling places within human astral bodies, and in a similar way the etheric body could also be plagued by ahrimanic beings.

But at that time Christ, when incarnated in a human body in Palestine, could heal only a few people, specifically *because* He was incarnated in a human body. Before He had overcome death through the Crucifixion and Resurrection, and had not yet descended into the 'I's of all human beings through the Mystery of Golgotha as seed of healing for the lower bodily sheaths, He had to work upon people from *without*. He could only stream His healing forces from outside into those whom He physically encountered in His physical body. While God, the Logos, did indeed live and work in this physical body, a healing could always only occur in direct personal encounter during these few months that He was active in Palestine.

Today, too, an illness is only really cured by Christ. But only since the Mystery of Golgotha does He work from *within* us, since He is no longer present on earth as an incarnate being whom only individual people can encounter. Today, earthly human beings must seek God the Son in themselves, and wage the battle against the adversarial powers through their own I – in which God the Son dwells. We can be entirely healed by conscious acknowledgement of the presence of Christ in us.

An example of the differing causes and course of illnesses at the time of Christ and today can be found in ordinary fever. What causes and effects did fever have at the dawn of the new era, and what are they today?

We know that fever is a luciferic gift. It drives up temperature in us, pushing us gradually towards excarnation. At the time of Christ, or rather before the Mystery of Golgotha, fever was also caused by Lucifer. However it led much more quickly to death than it does today. The reason why modern people generally cope better with fever than they did then lies in their I, which has awoken through the Christ impetus. Nowadays the I can gain control of and direct organic processes. It is today possible for the I to harness Lucifer for its purposes. This means that the I recognizes Lucifer's gift of fever as a highly effective tool for overcoming an illness: for driving out or compensating and redressing a different seed of illness — usually ahrimanic and thus 'cold' in nature — by the engendering of heat. Before the Mystery of Golgotha this was impossible, since the I could not yet produce the forces which it received through the Resurrection. In this example we see how the I forces can direct fever today — and thus also the course of various other accompanying illnesses, and how in fact Lucifer is compelled to serve the I. Today, therefore, fever is not necessarily to be regarded as an illness in itself but as a remedy against a real illness. From this one sees that the astral body must today be subordinate to the I — and the I is also in fact able to subordinate the astral body to itself through the forces of consciousness living in it, whereas at the time of Christ the still sleeping I was largely subject to the excesses of the astral body. In consequence healing could only occur from without, invoked by the I-bringer.

Faith and change of heart as precondition for healing at the time of Christ

There were two special criteria which had to be present for healing through the Christ to be lasting, or for Him to carry it out at all. The first is connected with the willingness of the heart to renew and care for the self that had fallen sick. The foundation for successful healing at the time of Christ was a deep inner longing for a healthy body, which the human being needed to develop in order to lead a life within it strengthened by faith. Christ was often heard to say: 'Your hearts are sick!' The soul which had fallen prey to all kinds of illness had to want to be well before the body could receive healing. The direct effect of a soul transgression, mostly coming to visible expression in an illness which could not be self-healed — that is, through the power of the individual's I — meant that the person concerned came to a certain insight into his illness. But as well as insight, which alone was not sufficient, there had to be an authentic desire for change in his own soul, and thus in his way of life.

Since the forces of consciousness of our own time were not yet available, such a process always came to expression in the kind of soul stance which we call faith in the spiritual world. People were not yet able to *know* the reality of the world of spirit, but they could believe — in fact they *had* to have such faith to create the foundation for healing their souls. Today, too, at an advanced level of development, the heart's willingness to transform the self is definitely necessary for illness sent by the good gods to lead to higher development. Will is the name for this willingness of the heart.

And thus, through the Gospels passed down to us, we can witness how Christ healed many people — thousands even — yet also dismissed those who did not approach Him in the right stance, who were unable to find faith and who had no wish to change their way of life. It may strike us as hard that the Lord did not heal everyone who approached Him: we have developed such an erroneous view of Christ that we think He could not have turned anyone away, since He epitomizes mercifulness. But here we overlook the fact that Christ's mercy consisted precisely in dismissing certain people without first liberating them from their sickness. Only in this way could He reflect back their true being to them, creating the basis for their hearts to be changed — which alone would lead to healing.

It was always the same picture: at the large-scale healings which He undertook, and to which hundreds of pilgrims flocked, there were also always those who complained and reproached Him, saying such things as: 'See, we returned today since the last time we came you did not heal us!' And they pointed to others and said: 'Why do you heal these, but not us?' Or others came who complained: 'Look at us! Last time you gave us your blessing, but we fell ill again!'* At this He turned to them and inscribed words in their souls embodied in a dynamic, pictorial image: 'Why do you not stretch out your arms to me?' This was easy to accomplish, and so they stretched out their arms to Him. But they failed to understand what He had meant by this. So He continued to speak: 'Why do you stretch out your arms to me in this way? Only because I said this to you? I do not see these arms which you stretch towards me. I see only the arms of your hearts, and as long as these are lifeless, I cannot and will not help you.' Then He added: 'You have no faith: you have

---

* These quotations are an attempt to give as faithful a translation as possible of words spoken by people in Christ's time, which the author heard them speak in her experiences of the events at the turning point of time.

doubt and are fickle.' With this saying Christ Jesus drew attention to the fact that such people were fundamentally not ready or willing to sunder themselves from their old lives, which had caused their illness. He could read their true state in their inner being. A good many of these people had led lives with which they were – unjustifiably – perfectly content, and secretly hoped after being healed by the 'miracle worker' to return to their old ways.

Secondly – and this was the other criterion underlying a healing – they had no faith. They were full of mistrust and doubt, and partly also fear and rejection of the Redeemer. They could not find in themselves the trust and conviction to see their salvation in Him. They had not recognized that in order to be healed their own participation was needed.

The Lord's disciples, too, first had to learn what true mercy was, and that it involved loving rigour as an aid to self-help. This was why, when they sometimes encountered another's dramatically poor state of health, they asked their Master: 'Do you have no pity on these people?' To this He replied in an equally strict, and irrevocably precise and clear way, which could be taken for severity or coldness by those who know nothing of the Son God's selfless mission of sacrifice for the human being. He described such people as the 'lukewarm' ones, clearly expressing the fact that He had not come to heal bodies so that sin could be indulged in them again without any conscience, and even in full pleasure. That was not why the Light of the World had come, nor was it the reason He had healed. He did not wish to heal these bodies so that sin could again take place in them.*

Methods for treating illnesses

The occult background to 'gout'

When Christ performed healings He did this in a particular and special way that specifically corresponded to the nature of the disease, yet the treatment of all those suffering from the same illness did not seem to vary depending on the individual. At the dawn of the new era, clinical pictures always manifested in very clearly defined forms, still corresponding to the

---

* See Rudolf Steiner's last address dated 28 September 1924 in: *Karmic Relationships*, Vol. IV (op. cit.).

ILLNESS AND HEALING AT THE TIME OF CHRIST 75

group-soul condition of human beings and having identical causes. Two people who were deaf were almost invariably both deaf for the same reason. We can imagine this in really very simple terms: the same kind of transgression produced the same illness in two different people. Methods of treatment, however, differed depending on the type of illness.

During the days when Christ Jesus was speaking to a large crowd of people — instructing them in everything from the simplest matters of conduct through to spiritual teachings — healings were also performed after He had spoken; or the Lord spent several days alone at a certain place — usually in the Galilean landscape — solely to allow the sick to come to Him. Great numbers came. The word went round like wildfire that incomparable powers could take effect in Jesus of Nazareth. Though He spoke to them in an unaccustomed mode, His words resonated in their souls in a strangely familiar and profoundly truthful way. It was said that people could even be healed by His words alone, and since then they had been wholly seized and fired by new hope, confidence and life.

For the sick, as also for their relatives or companions, the personal encounter with the Redeemer was life-changing and fateful. His high being grasped hold of the whole person who encountered Him, in infinite gravity and unshakeable esteem. Never before had these people experienced such attentiveness, nor such an overwhelming sense of their own being's uniqueness, rightness and beauty. Thus many were already in a transformed state and receptive to the reality of the spirit when He began to heal their illness.

Mostly He first directed His gaze to the face of the sick person, sought to encounter him, until their looks met: the sick person would then be deeply, inwardly moved in the way just described. Then Christ would direct His attention to the affected part or organ. He nearly always spoke quietly to the patient, in a very reflective, even tender tone, at the same time, or just afterwards, performing special gestures which drove forces out of the sick body, or brought them into harmony.

If the person suffered from deafness, He seemed to incline His head closely to his ear and, instead of speaking words to him, to breathe His divine breath into him.

ILLNESS AND HEALING AT THE TIME OF CHRIST 77

When someone with gout or 'palsy'* was brought to Him, He approached them in a different way. The gout usually affected the spine, arms, legs or joints. In the case of the spine, He stroked once, gently, along its length, whereas for someone suffering from gout in the joints, He took hold of the joints and shook them – giving a tangible sense of the way in which this shook off the gout.

If we use spiritual-scientific means to look at this kind of treatment for gout, we can discover that, for example, shaking out the arms was the only really effective way to heal gout in the arms, for it directly engaged with what had triggered the disease. The gout manifesting in arms, hands and joints was always caused by avarice or theft – a deed motivated by greed. The astral driving force for avarice, and the robbery it led to, intervened destructively as soul-spiritual entity in the body's organization. When the greed of an avaricious person strove for the possessions of others, his impurity of soul spread out its astral element like arms and hands. And the degree of soul impurity, or

---

*This is the word given in the Matthew Gospel (King James version) which is referred to as 'gout' (*Gicht*) in the German Martin Luther Bible. (Translator's note.)

even the amount of goods stolen, ultimately corresponded precisely to the severity of his illness. The avaricious soul motivation, the spiritual worth of what was stolen, lodged itself in the joints and made it impossible for people to move their limbs. From then on they would drag around with them their astral drives rigidified into sensory reality. If the person affected gained insight into his transgressions and was ready for a different way of life, and came before Christ Jesus, the burden of his sins really did fall from him as his arms were shaken, and with it the occult freight of the stolen goods which he had once made off with.

The occult background to 'possession'

The healing of those possessed took place in a different way. In some cases the Lord visited the sick at home, or they were brought to Him. It could also happen that the demon wreaking havoc in a person would only become outwardly manifest if it was met with an entirely opposite impetus, such as that from the Christ Himself. In contrast to the healing of blind, mute or deaf people, or those with gout, the Lord always maintained a clear distance from those possessed. This certainly was not for the reason proposed by the priests, that of potential pollution, but such distance appeared on the one hand to increase the effectiveness of His treatment, and on the other His proximity could have torn apart the physical dwelling of souls plagued by demons. The encounter of a demon with the Christ being could therefore not take place within someone's physical body or in its direct periphery. The demon literally had to be driven out, and thus Christ Jesus did not speak gently to such a person but with a mighty, thundering voice.

When a demon of this kind finally emerged, the person whom it had possessed collapsed into himself as though struck by lightning. Those who had been treated usually fell into a deep sleep or faint, and when they awoke from this they seemed to be in agony and thoroughly taken up with what had occurred in them, remaining exhausted by it for several more days. It is understandable that after being healed from such an illness a person would need to sleep for days on end to recover. He might, after all, have been possessed by an evil spirit for years, have been driven by it, and continually active in its service, and was now terribly fatigued by all such enforced activity. We could compare this with the image of a puppet collapsing the moment the strings are cut which previously moved it. Thus it was possible to observe that, basically, almost none of those healed spontaneously leapt up afterwards and ran around cheerfully. What had been performed was not some kind of empty magic, but the alleviation of a complex condition that had weakened the organism over a long period. After a certain time of convalescence the 'puppet' needed to become a self-determining human being once more who, after the illness was driven out of him, gradually had to re-acquire his physical capacities such as sight, hearing or speech.

The nature of the possessed condition, which was common at the dawn of the new era, can be clarified by a passage in the Gospels. Below I try to give a tangible sense of how what unfolds in our I-governed souls today as inner conflict used to manifest outwardly in the clinical picture of possession.

To better understand the process at work in the soul of a possessed person, I will cite two passages which report the same scene: firstly as described by Mark and secondly by Luke; for only by conflating these two descriptions – even if they show only slight nuances of difference — can we gain insight into this state.

> *And they went into Capernaum; and straightway on the sabbath day he entered into the synagogue, and taught. And they were astonished at his doctrine: for he taught them as one that had authority, and not as the scribes. And there was in their synagogue a man with an unclean spirit; and he cried out, saying, Let us alone; what have we to do with thee, thou Jesus of Nazareth? art thou come to destroy us? I know thee who thou art, the Holy One of God. And Jesus rebuked him, saying, Hold thy peace, and come out of him. And when the unclean spirit had torn him, and cried with a loud voice, he came out of him.* (Mark 1, 21–26)

> *And he came down to Capernaum, a city of Galilee, and taught them on the sabbath days. And they were astonished at his doctrine: for his word was with power. And in the synagogue there was a man, which had a spirit of an unclean devil, and cried out with a loud voice, saying, Let us alone; what have we to do with thee, thou Jesus of Nazareth? art thou come to destroy us? I know thee who thou art; the Holy One of*

> *God. And Jesus rebuked him, saying, Hold thy peace, and come out of him. And when the devil had thrown him in the midst, he came out of him, and hurt him not.* (Luke 4, 31-35)

The first thing to say is that the 'power' mentioned in the Luke version above has nothing to do with obduracy or mere strength. Instead this expresses the direct experience people had of Christ's words being imbued with true life. His speech had nothing theoretical about it, like that of the learned scribes, but was fired by the presence of the living spirit. They did not hear *about* something in the ordinary form of a discourse, but instead they experienced what was spoken as breathing, spiritual reality. This is what the word 'power' indicates. No one could speak as powerfully as the Word itself, which was with God in the beginning and now was revealed in the body of Jesus of Nazareth on earth. And this power of the word of God was made apparent by the way it drove the demon out.

In reality, however, two different demons were involved here and had taken possession of the visitor to the synagogue. While Mark and Luke both speak of *one* demon, the subsequent account of the scene indicates the precise circumstances of the illness. Unlike many people of those times who had a sense of the different nature, the authenticity of Christ, but did not consciously recognize Him for what He was, the evil spirits Lucifer and Ahriman immediately recognized the Master of the higher worlds and saw Him as endangering their activity, as a risk to their adversarial existence: 'Art thou come to destroy us? We know thee who thou art; the Holy One of God.' The demon voice speaks of itself here in the 'we' form, that is, from the perspective of the fallen spirits Lucifer and Ahriman, and on behalf of those synagogue visitors present who are also possessed by the impure spirits.

The duality* of the demon is also very vividly expressed in the description of the Evangelist Mark, where he writes: 'And when the unclean spirit had torn him...' Between two extremes we are torn back and forth, paralyzed and rendered passive, so that we

---

* The German version given here speaks of the man being shaken 'back and forth', which is not reproduced in the King James version. In other versions in English, however, the word 'convulsions' is used, which better reflects the author's point in the following passage. (Translator's note.)

become incapable of maintaining self-control. This formulation shows the human soul condition in which, without the balancing, Trinitarian and mediating power of Christ, we find ourselves caught between the polarities of Lucifer and Ahriman. The influx of the Christ impetus into the human being always mediates between these two dark forces, placing itself between them as a wholesome and healing soul element and, by bringing the polarities back into equilibrium, not only halts their destructive power but also leads them towards redemption.

If you go to the Goetheanum at Dornach, Switzerland, to see the large wooden carving the Representative of Humanity, as He stands there between Lucifer and Ahriman, and allow its effect to work upon you, you can gain a sense of that inner arena of conflict which daily unfolds within each of us; and one can rediscover this same dynamic in the scene of the healing of the possessed man. At the dawn of the new era, before the I forces could take hold of and inform the inner soul, these forces were taught to the human being from without, by Christ. In the 'Group' statue we see a depiction of the polar forces of Lucifer and Ahriman alongside the Representative of Humanity, as these take shape in the human soul. This is why Rudolf Steiner did not always just refer to the figure in the carving as 'Christ', but rather as the 'Representative of Humanity': He represents us by standing in inwardly wrestling interaction with, and mediation between, the dark forces. Thus, in a lecture given in Basel three months after the first Goetheanum was burned down, Rudolf Steiner said:

> *A nine-metre-high sculptural group carved in wood, in which the Representative of Humanity is depicted as Christ standing between the temptations of Ahriman and Lucifer, aims to serve as something which encapsulates everything that lived as forms and all that could ever have been spoken or artistically represented in the Goetheanum.**

This temptation is however held at bay by the Christ being, sculpturally expressed in the fall of Lucifer above the central figure, and the constraining of Ahriman below Him. This central figure is thus a reflection of our inner life which, tempted and torn hither and thither between Ahriman and Lucifer, can

---
* Rudolf Steiner: *Was sollte das Goetheanum and was soll die Anthroposophie?* (GA 84), lecture of 9 April 1923.

find a healing, balanced core of being by invoking the Christ power concealed in us. This can illumine what Luke writes: 'And when the devil had thrown him in the midst, he came out of him, and hurt him not.' At the moment of liberation through the mediating power of the I, the demons must relinquish the human being, throwing him back into the midst or centre of himself. We fall literally into ourselves, coming 'to ourselves' and thus remaining in our own 'midst'.*

This is the true Michaelic battle that must today generally be waged within us. The prime thing here is not so much to accuse others of their un-Michaelic conduct but rather to examine ourselves. The battle should not be waged *between* people — irrespective of how misguided or jeopardized one person may consider another. First and foremost this battle takes place in our own soul, and it is there that it may and must be waged in the most stringent and unwavering way, day after day. Thus Michael helps us to fulfil Christ's mission to the human world.

---

*In the King James version, and most other versions, translators stumble over this passage, assuming it refers to the physical 'midst' of the synagogue or the other people observing. (Translator's note.)

*Healing the possessed man, circa 968, ivory carving.
Hessisches Landmuseum, Darmstadt*

Christ healing a bleeding woman, early Christian art, no later than 3rd century AD, fresco.
Cimitero di SS Marcelino e Piertro, Rome

*Healing the leper, Byzantine school, 12th century, mosaic.
Duomo Monreale, Sicily*

Healing the daughter of Jairus, painting by George Percy Hood (1857–1930). Guildhall Art Gallery, London

The healing of the man with dropsy

Let us now turn to another illness and its cause, which the Gospels refer to as 'dropsy'. In the case of this disease the luciferic forces which possessed the astral body concluded a malign pact with the ahrimanic ones raging in the etheric body. At the time of Christ this alliance expressed itself in the clinical picture of dropsy in the human being's physical body. What occurred in the human body to trigger this disease? Dropsy arose when the fluid balance between blood and tissue was disturbed; and this displacement of the etheric balance in the body's fluids was an expression of the action of ahrimanic powers. Today, likewise, we find similar illnesses in the form of oedemas or so-called ascites. If too much fluid emerges from the blood for it to be absorbed by the body or transported away by the lymph, build-up of fluid occurs at tissue sites, tissue junctions or cavities — i.e. at places where it does not belong. One could see how people with dropsy who were brought to the Saviour had swollen eyes, and their stomachs were also often very swollen since the water had settled in the abdominal cavity. At this point the astral body responded to the displacement of the etheric body, giving rise in part to painful inflammations, nerve pains and, following a kind of excess cooling, ultimately to fever, which the luciferic activity invoked.

The Lord treated those with dropsy by laying His hands on them. He placed His left hand on their head, forehead or face, while His right hand rested on their solar plexus. Then He said: 'Through the right hand Joachim works in you. Through the left hand Boas works in you; and they stand before your temple so that your spirit enters it through them!'*

With these mantric words and this healing gesture, He engendered a flow of forces, a current of energy which pulled in Ahriman and pushed away Lucifer, thus leading the bodily sheaths in which these were exerting a malign influence back into equilibrium. Thus He mediated between solar plexus activity and nerve-head activity; and the re-creation of balance between these two forces in the human body manifested in the fact that the excess fluid was excreted through the skin in a spontaneous and heavy flow of perspiration from swollen eyelids, faces, eye sockets

---

* See Rudolf Steiner's last address dated 28 September 1924 in: *Karmic Relationships*, Vol. IV (op. cit.).

and the abdominal cavity. This meant a huge relief for the patient — here again a burden was lifted from him as balance was re-established in the system of super-sensible bodies.

The healing of the woman with the issue of blood, and the raising of the daughter of Jairus

All healings, of whatever illness, were only possible if the condition of 'faith' was fulfilled. This did not involve a belief in miracles, and certainly not the idea that human beings might have anything they desire if they only believe in it, for such faith would really only be presumption or fantasy. The faith involved in the stories of healing indeed testifies to the secret of overcoming personal will in favour of the divine will. Christ always spoke to human beings who could come to healing through Him: 'Daughter, thy faith hath made thee whole.' Or: 'Great is thy faith: be it unto thee even as thou wilt.' But whoever could not have selfless faith in Him, and was interested only in his own benefit, by whatever means, could either not be healed at all or not enduringly. In contrast to these doubters, unfaithful or 'self-willed' people, we hear of the healing of the leper as follows:

> *And it came to pass, when he was in a certain city, behold a man full of leprosy: who seeing Jesus fell on his face, and besought him, saying, Lord, if thou wilt, thou canst make me clean. And he [Jesus] put forth his hand, and touched him, saying, I will: be thou clean. And immediately the leprosy departed from him.* (Luke 5, 12–13)

This can remind us of the night on the Mount of Olives, in which the Son Himself says: 'Father, if thou be willing, remove this cup from me: nevertheless not my will, but thine, be done. And there appeared an angel unto him from heaven, strengthening him' (Luke 22, 42–43).

In this context we should also mention the story of the woman with the issue of blood, who had already given away all her money to pay for consultations with many different doctors, without any alleviation of her condition. Only once she had given away all her material goods could she come to faith, as I have described it above:

> *And, behold, a woman, which was diseased with an issue of blood twelve years, came behind him, and*

ILLNESS AND HEALING AT THE TIME OF CHRIST

> *touched the hem of his garment: For she said within herself, If I may but touch his garment, I shall be whole. But Jesus turned him about, and when he saw her, he said, Daughter, be of good comfort; thy faith hath made thee whole. And the woman was made whole from that hour.* (Matthew 9, 20–22)

But now I would like to examine this passage in more detail, for it occupies a very special place among the stories of healing. It actually prepares the disciples for a gradual understanding of the raising of Lazarus. The woman with the issue of blood is mentioned as though in one breath with the raising of the daughter of Jairus. This is by no means accidental; and once again we must decipher the Mystery language of the Gospels to arrive at an understanding of the connection between the woman with the issue of blood and the raising of the daughter of Jairus. For this reason, I will quote the whole Gospel passage, in the version by Mark, which describes the events with great precision:

> *And when Jesus was passed over again by ship unto the other side,* [and here we can recall what was said previously about the meaning of the 'other side'] *much people gathered unto him: and he was*

nigh unto the sea. And, behold, there cometh one of the rulers of the synagogue, Jairus by name; and when he saw him, he fell at his feet, And besought him greatly, saying, My little daughter lieth at the point of death: I pray thee, come and lay thy hands on her, that she may be healed; and she shall live. And Jesus went with him; and much people followed him, and thronged him.

And a certain woman, which had an issue of blood twelve years, And had suffered many things of many physicians, and had spent all that she had, and was nothing bettered, but rather grew worse, When she had heard of Jesus, came in the press behind, and touched his garment. For she said, If I may touch but his clothes, I shall be whole. And straightway the fountain of her blood was dried up; and she felt in her body that she was healed of that plague. And Jesus, immediately knowing in himself that virtue had gone out of him, turned him about in the press, and said, Who touched my clothes? And his disciples said unto him, Thou seest the multitude thronging thee, and sayest thou, Who touched me? And he looked round about to see her that had done this thing. But the woman fearing and trembling, know-

ing what was done in her, came and fell down before him, and told him all the truth. And he said unto her, Daughter, thy faith hath made thee whole; go in peace, and be whole of thy plague.

While he yet spake, there came from the ruler of the synagogue's house certain which said, Thy daughter is dead: why troublest thou the Master any further? As soon as Jesus heard the word that was spoken, he saith unto the ruler of the synagogue, Be not afraid, only believe. And he suffered no man to follow him, save Peter, and James, and John the brother of James. And he cometh to the house of the ruler of the synagogue, and seeth the tumult, and them that wept and wailed greatly. And when he was come in, he saith unto them, Why make ye this ado, and weep? the damsel is not dead, but sleepeth. And they laughed him to scorn. But when he had put them all out, he taketh the father and the mother of the damsel, and them that were with him, and entereth in where the damsel was lying. And he took the damsel by the hand, and said unto her, Talitha cumi; which is, being interpreted, Damsel, I say unto thee, arise. And straightway the damsel arose, and walked; for she was of the age of twelve years. And they were

> *astonished with a great astonishment. And he charged them straitly that no man should know it; and commanded that something should be given her to eat.* (Mark 5, 21–43)

It was the cosmic power of Christ that was able to perform the healings in Jesus of Nazareth. Thus the human being Jesus felt a flow of strength emanating from him which healed the woman with the issue of blood. And as Christ Jesus turned around and asked who had touched Him, his disciples failed to grasp what He meant, or why He asked such a question. This question did not express His own enquiry or even lack of knowledge, but instead sought a profession of faith from the woman with the issue of blood. And when she stepped forwards and *told him all the truth,* He said: 'Daughter, thy faith hath made thee whole; go in peace, and be whole of thy plague.' At this moment the woman experienced the reality of divine will, just as the Son experienced this during the night on the Mount of Olives. Only when the woman uttered a profession of faith drawn from within herself could she be lastingly healed from her suffering.

We also hear that the daughter of Jairus had not yet died when the woman with the issue of blood approached the Redeemer. He was on His way to the sick child when the incident with the woman with the issue of blood occurred. The woman was released from her suffering at the same moment that the child died, for the Gospel tells us that: 'While he yet spake, there came from the ruler of the synagogue's house certain which said, Thy daughter is dead...' Apart from this apparently chance connection between the time of the healing of the woman and the death of the girl, and apart from a further suggestion which I will examine in a moment, a superficial consideration will find scarcely anything to show that the story of healing and that of the raising are indeed interwoven in both a destined and causative sense. We have to examine various aspects together to gain an overall picture of the link between these two events, for their comprehensive significance cannot be understood without considering other circumstances. We will therefore need to stay mentally flexible and make a few conceptual leaps before the separate parts can form a whole.

For example, we must add here that one phenomenon of the pre-Christian era was that illnesses could be transferred to children in a particular way. More precisely, an illness in a child could be caused by an adult's failing. I am not talking of bacterial or viral infections as we know them today, but a soul infection. One or both parents could transgress in some way, but their child would fall ill instead of them. This affected the members of the tribe of Israel particularly severely – still more severely than if the person himself, as adult, had fallen ill. The people of Israel who, since the time of their forefather Abraham, had lived in a seamless sense of generational continuity, as preparation for the physical body of the Messiah, placed the very greatest value on their offspring. Today we can have scarcely any idea of what people felt at the time when denied the blessing of children. This was not about the fulfilment of personal ideas and wishes connected with one's own descendants, as is generally the case today. Rooted wholly in the context of the nation and race, members of the ancient Hebrew people saw their descendants as an indispensable link in the chain of generations leading to the arrival of the Messiah.

The chief of the synagogue, Jairus, had in fact

ILLNESS AND HEALING AT THE TIME OF CHRIST

sinned, and this led to his child falling ill. His misdemeanour had occurred exactly twelve years before the meeting with Christ, and at his daughter's birth this sin had been implanted in the child as the germ of an illness.

We find a concealed hint of the cause of this in the description of the moment when the woman with the issue of blood comes to Jairus's house, which Christ is about to enter. The passage says: 'And Jesus went with him [Jairus]; and much people followed him, and thronged him. And a certain woman, which had an issue of blood twelve years ... and had spent all that she had, and was nothing bettered, but rather grew worse.'

There was in fact a connection between the illness of the woman with the issue of blood and the illness of Jairus's daughter.

This woman with the issue of blood had once been extremely prosperous before she fell ill, possessing great wealth and many estates. This prosperity had spoiled her however, and one day she sinned as follows. At the time it was common to ask the scribes, priests or rabbis for their advice in all kinds of situations, chiefly however in relation to questions of the law or its interpretation. But this once highly honourable practice had degenerated into an empty habit, comparable with the public prayer which Jesus attacked, and which mainly served as a show to others of one's supposed piety. It was the same with the custom of seeking advice, for by then it was much less to do with getting a wise person's view than with showing one's neighbours how seriously one took the religious laws. The more often one was seen to confer with the rabbi, the more important one's standing became in Jewish circles, and the more one's (probably already amassed) prosperity was associated with a certain position in the religious domain. This could give someone the aura of an elevated person whose influence, enhanced by his familiarity with a servant of God, could assume grand proportions.

Twelve years before her encounter with Christ, this same woman had committed a sin with the chief of the synagogue. Both had sinned. She had sent him a considerable sum of money so that he could arrange for her as many meetings with the local rabbi as possible. He had accepted the money and given her dates for the meetings. By doing this, both she and the chief of the synagogue gained an advantage over others who sought advice, who might well have been in much greater need of the rabbi's help but did not have the necessary financial means to gain access to him. Then the young daughter of Jairus fell ill in consequence of her father's guilt, and the prosperous woman fell ill with the issue of blood. The money she had paid out, and let 'issue forth' for selfish purposes, matched the outpouring of her blood: the elixir bearing her I that was seeking to awaken. And the more she paid for medical consultations, the greater became her suffering.

Both illnesses — that of the woman and of the child — had grown continually worse up to the twelfth year, until the child was close to death. And both in the woman and in Jairus, 'earthly assets', in the sense both of money and strength, had to come to an end so that they might turn to Christ and recognize Him. The woman had to be bereft of all her wealth and property, and the synagogue chief had to see that he had implanted the seed of death in his daughter, and that now only the Son of God could help.

The Lord urged the woman to make acknowledgement of this when He turned round and asked who had touched Him. And He drew on Jairus's faith, although the latter had just been told that his daughter had died and that now his plea to Jesus was in vain. The Lord ignored these words and said: 'Be not afraid, only believe.'

For the first time, Jairus was shown who Jesus of Nazareth really was through the fact that the child had to enter death so as to be brought back to life by Christ. Only through the raising of his daughter did he grasp that the child must live — but no longer for the sake of the sequence of generations, for the Christ already stood in their midst. Thus, through the raising of his daughter, Jairus recognized the bodily reality and presence of the Messiah.

But this scene also conceals within it an intimation of the raising of Lazarus which — in contrast to the raising of Jairus's daughter which preceded and prepared it — was to take place in full public view, and which itself was a preparation for understanding Christ's deed of sacrifice on Golgotha and the Mystery of the Resurrection.

The raising of Lazarus unites in *one* figure what is still divided between two people — that is, woman and child — as cause and effect in the raising of the daughter of Jairus and the healing of the woman with the issue of blood. The child had to die away from an old state or condition, so that all impurity departed from her, just as the woman had to relinquish all her wealth to become whole. She did not become whole because she spent all her wealth on costly treatments but, on the contrary, she only regained her health when she no longer had any means to fall back on. But since she had not spent her assets for selfless purposes, but had given a considerable portion to Jairus, the latter's daughter had to enter death. Thus are interwoven the destinies and stories of the healing of the woman with the issue of blood and the raising of the daughter of Jairus, which only the deed of Christ resolves so that the two are released from each other.

Before he was raised, Lazarus too had not wanted to relinquish his belongings, which is what led to him falling ill. We first hear how the rich disciple threw himself at the feet of the Lord and asked how he might attain eternal life. After Christ Jesus had imposed on him adherence to the Commandments of Moses, and the latter had assured Him that he had always adhered to them since his youth, the Gospel says:

> *Then Jesus beholding him loved him* [an indication of the identity of the disciple whom 'the Lord loved'], *and said unto him, One thing thou lackest: go thy way, sell whatsoever thou hast, and give to the poor, and thou shalt have treasure in heaven: and come, take up the cross, and follow me. And he was sad at that saying, and went away grieved: for he had great possessions.* (Mark 10, 21-22)

And thus it finally happened that this rich disciple, Lazarus of Bethany, fell ill, since he did not wish to relinquish his property: 'Therefore his sisters sent unto him, saying, Lord, behold, he whom thou lovest is sick' (John 11, 3). But, similar to the raising of the daughter of Jairus, when the Lord said: 'And all wept, and bewailed her: but he said, Weep not; she is not dead, but sleepeth' (Luke 8, 52), He now proclaimed: 'This sickness is not unto death, but for the glory of God, that the Son of God might be glorified thereby' (John 11, 4).

This meant that death should have no power over

those who follow Christ. The 'first' death,* that of matter, is to have no further power over the life of the soul. The spiritual human being is to be given the power to pass unharmed through death. Rudolf Steiner expressed this in the mantric phrase: 'In Christ death becomes life.'† Whoever is in Christ will experience how death turns to life. But the Christ, the Word become flesh, is the awoken I in the human being, which, from the core of our being, says: I AM.

Thus Christ speaks to Martha, the sister of Lazarus: 'Jesus said unto her, I AM the resurrection, and the life: he that believeth in me, though he were dead, yet shall he live: And whosoever liveth and believeth in me shall never die. Believest thou this?'

And then we hear the overwhelming profession of faith: 'Yea, Lord: I believe that thou art the Christ, the Son of God, which should come into the world' (John 11, 25–27).

---

* See also: 'Blessed and holy is he that hath part in the first resurrection: on such the second death hath no power...' (Revelations 20, 6) and '...death and hell were cast into the lake of fire. This is the second death' (Revelations 20, 14).
† See Rudolf Steiner's Foundation Stone verse.

Apart from Martha, Peter is the only other one whom we hear speak with such clarity: 'Thou art the Christ, the Son of the living God' (Matthew 16, 16). Such acknowledgement and profession of faith is only possible because Christ lived among human beings on earth in a human body. He thus becomes manifest in earthly space, whereas previously He was only perceptible in cosmic worlds. This profession by Peter, which is given somewhat differently in the Gospel of John, also contains a reference that substantiates a statement by Rudolf Steiner. 'Lord ... thou hast the words of eternal life [i.e. 'you are the Word of eternal life']. And we believe and are sure that thou art that Christ, the Son of the living God. Jesus answered them, Have not I chosen you twelve...' (John 6, 68–70).

Only through Christ being revealed and manifest on earth, that is, in physical space, is space itself permeated with Christ, and this revelation of the Christ in physical space is reflected in the number 12. In a lecture on 30 August 1909,* Rudolf Steiner points to the fact that wherever the number twelve appears Christ is no longer revealed only in time but also in space. Where

---

* Rudolf Steiner: *The East in the Light of the West* (Garber Communications 1986), lecture of 30 August 1909.

the number twelve arises, he says, time flows into space. And this manifestation in space is a reflection of planetary space on the physical plane, which the Christ brought with Him when He entered the 'earthly stream of life' from the stream of time.* Therefore Christ emerges from the midst of the twelve tribes of Israel and chooses twelve disciples: 'Have not I chosen you twelve...' Exactly twelve years had passed since the woman with the issue of blood fell ill when He became manifest to her, the parents of the girl and His three disciples whom He took with him into the chamber of Jairus's daughter. The apparently unimportant remark, 'And straightway the damsel arose, and walked; for she was of the age of twelve years', can now appear to us in a new, significant light.

Christ's instructions to the healed

However, only each individual, through his own insight, can arrive at this faith, this acknowledgement

---

* See Rudolf Steiner's Foundation Stone verse: 'At the turning point of time / The Spirit Light of the World / Entered the Stream of Earthly Being.'

of the revelation of Christ on the physical plane. And this was also why no mass healings took place. While it is true that many sick people came to the Saviour at once, each one was treated separately and individually. Thus treatment was always a matter of a person turning personally to Christ, and vice versa.

This is why we read in the Gospels that, unlike the raising of Lazarus, the raising of the daughter of Jairus occurred solely in the presence of her parents and three of the disciples. The raising of the daughter of Jairus had on the one hand to take place before her parents' eyes since they were responsible for causing her illness. On the other hand, Peter, James and John were also there. At this point it becomes clear that there must have been a particular reason for their presence.

I have previously suggested that these three disciples stand in an accentuated relationship with the Christ Mystery;* that — some time after the raising of the daughter of Jairus — they accompany the Lord to Mount Tabor and become witnesses of His Trans-

---

* See Judith von Halle: *And If He Has Not Been Raised* (Temple Lodge Publishing 2007), in the chapter entitled: 'The Transfiguration on Mount Tabor and the last night on the Mount of Olives'.

figuration; and that it is they who finally, in the last hours before His arrest, hear from close proximity His occult dialogue with God the Father and witness His struggle with the adversarial powers.

Here we should be aware that the 'John' who both witnesses the raising of the daughter of Jairus and the Transfiguration of Christ is the one also called 'little' John — in other words the younger brother of James son of Zebedee — whereas the one who witnessed the night on the Mount of Olives and the Mystery of Golgotha is the Evangelist and thus Lazarus-John, as Rudolf Steiner described him. This fundamental connection is an integral part of the Mystery of Lazarus-John and — when the time for this arrives — should be fully illumined and clarified since it is a question of great significance for humanity. Until such time, however, we cannot avoid seeing a connection between these two people, and it must be emphasized that there were good reasons why 'little' John not only witnessed the Transfiguration on Mount Tabor but also the raising of the daughter of Jairus. The teaching which John Zebedee received passed, in fact, into the being of Lazarus-John. And thus, at the raising of the daughter of Jairus, John heard the same phrase in Aramaic as he would hear at the raising of Lazarus: '*Thalita kumi!*' — and, finally: '*Laza'ár kumi!*'

In a special way, therefore, the Redeemer allowed Peter, James and John to share in the Mystery of His transformation. He prepared them intentionally for the secret of the Resurrection of Easter Sunday. Watching the raising of the daughter of Jairus — with the public excluded — served to instruct the three as a preparation for the Lazarus Mystery, which would concern John Zebedee in particular.

The raising of Lazarus was performed in the presence of a large crowd of people, so that as many as possible could be prepared for the forthcoming Crucifixion and Resurrection of God in human form, and later might gain insight into the divine identity of the crucified Christ Jesus:

> *Then they took away the stone from the place where the dead was laid. And Jesus lifted up his eyes, and said, Father, I thank thee that thou hast heard me. And I knew that thou hearest me always: but because*

> *of the people which stand by I said it, that they may believe that thou hast sent me. And when he thus had spoken, he cried with a loud voice, Lazarus, come forth.* (John 11, 41–43)

In contrast to this, the raising of the daughter of Jairus, which occurred around two years before the Lazarus Mystery, was – as emphasized already – only performed in front of the three disciples and the parents involved. The Lord also imposed strict secrecy about the divine source of His deed both on the parents of the raised daughter and even on His disciples. The others were not meant to hear of this from witnesses, or be convinced of His coming by hearsay and rumour, but should recognize Him *themselves*. We repeatedly hear the warnings the Lord issued after He had performed a healing:

> *And he charged them straitly that no man should know it* (Mark 5, 43). *And he straitly charged them that they should not make him known* (Mark 3, 12). *And Jesus saith unto him, See thou tell no man; but go thy way...* (Matthew 8, 4). *And ... Jesus straitly charged them, saying, See that no man know it.* (Matthew 9, 30).

These warnings were always preceded by the sick person's profession of faith, such as this one: 'Thou art the Son of God' (Mark 3,11). The command to keep His identity concealed was due to the need for each person to come to individual knowledge of Christ. Before the Mystery of Golgotha, the Christ could only reveal Himself in the individual people whom He encountered.

But we may doubt how such individual knowledge was possible if on some days many were healed rather than individual people; and when it even says:

> *But Jesus withdrew himself with his disciples to the sea: and a great multitude from Galilee followed him, and from Judaea, And from Jerusalem, and from Idumaea, and from beyond Jordan; and they about Tyre and Sidon, a great multitude...* (Mark 3, 7–8) *... and he healed them, And charged them that they should not make him known...* (Matthew 12, 15–16).

This might lead us to the mistaken view that it must basically have been completely pointless to command a whole crowd to keep silent about Him. But in fact He never spoke such words to the crowd, and always only to a single individual.

I have already stated that it was characteristic of conditions prevailing in those times, and of the nature of the human being then, that Christ Jesus always treated sick people with the same illness in the same way, since, due to the general influence of Lucifer and Ahriman on the pre-Christian world, the causes of each illness were likewise the same. Once the cause of an illness had been eradicated, however, and its destructive effects on the physical body had been healed, the Redeemer always turned to address each person in an individual way. Following the autonomous profession of faith by an individual, a brief, confidential conversation always took place. In these discussions, quietly and concealed from others' eyes and ears, the Lord would impart to each person instructions that were specifically for him. Those close by became as if deaf and blind at such moments. As if raised out of time, this event occurred only between two human 'I's: between Christ Jesus and the one who had been healed. These few but significant words, directed exclusively to the individual, were inaudible to all others for whom they were not intended. Thus only the last phrase which the Lord spoke to each has been passed down to us: 'Do not reveal me to the others!' He was only to be perceived through the individual core of being of each person.

The Lord urged each person He healed to 'sin no more!' He warned them all against sinning again in the same way as previously, since otherwise their illness would return: 'Behold, thou art made whole: sin no more, lest a worse thing come unto thee' (John 5, 14). And this is precisely what happened to those who did not follow His advice — they fell ill again. He gave the individual instructions which followed each healing in order to offer those who had been healed — who were still at risk as before — a practical aid in defending themselves against temptations by demons. These were mantric words, appropriate to the conditions of those times, in the form of parables or prayers. The Lord urged them to remember these words. If one wished to translate them into our language, one would have to formulate them roughly as follows: 'Bear this within you until such day as you will behold the whole glory of the Son of the Father.'

ILLNESS AND HEALING AT THE TIME OF CHRIST 113

In giving mantric words and prayers, and urging also that people should absorb these, Christ Jesus enabled those He healed to remain pure in a direct and practical way, until the Redeemer should have overcome all sickness and death for them and all humanity.

If we think back to the general condition of humanity shortly before the Mystery of Golgotha, as sketched in Fig. 2 (page 61), we can gain a tangible sense of the reason for giving special mantra and prayers and urging people to remember these. The empty sheaths of the gods' dwelling places, which the human being had brought with him in his astral body through the succession of cultural epochs, had progressively been occupied by demons, and these could exert particularly destructive effects if the human being, by leading an immoral life, supplied these demons with improvident astral nourishment. At the moment a healing was performed and Christ had driven these demons out of the bodies of sick people, these sheaths of the dwelling places of the gods remained behind in an empty state, cleansed of the adversarial beings. Thus they were empty, and each person needed to fill them with something new to prevent them being re-occupied by the luciferic and ahrimanic spirits. He was therefore to fill them with the prayers and esoteric exercises which Christ Jesus had given him, until the day when he would *behold the whole glory of the Son of the Father*; in other words, until the Mystery of Golgotha, when the divine spirit would itself enter and inhabit these sheaths of his body.

Sometimes those who had been healed asked the Lord: 'Should we now go to John and be baptized?' But He replied: 'Go your ways and sin no more; and be baptized by my disciples when the time has come.'* By saying this He was instructing them to keep their bodily sheaths pure until the disciples should baptize them with the divine spirit, with the fire of the Holy Ghost and not with water, so that this fiery spirit could then fill the sheaths of their physical existence.†

---

* See footnote on page 72.
† Irrespective of this, the baptism of John was indispensable insofar as John used it to prepare those people for the encounter with Christ who had not yet come into contact with Him. Thus John's baptism prepared the human being to accept what Christ would ultimately bring.

Thus the process of separating from the astral plane, as this has been described, and the resulting entry of the adversarial forces into the human being, was one intrinsically interwoven with the great, divine plan. While in those long-gone times the human being lost his direct contact with the divine world, those empty sheaths *had to* arise in his body so that they could eventually be filled with the Christ element. Today, in the age of the consciousness soul, we are turning towards the world of the gods in a new way. Through the power of our consciousness awoken into the world of spirit, we are now able to bear planetary forces down into those formerly empty sheaths – the dwelling places of the gods – enabling the gods themselves to enter us again. Thus the microcosm does not go out into and merge with the macrocosm, but instead the macrocosm enters the microcosm, as was prefigured by the descent of the Logos to the earth. We can bring this about by transposing ourselves into the world of spirit without sundering ourselves from our earthly, physical body. In and around ourselves we build the temple of the spiritual human being, and fetch the world of the gods into the inner self.

The healing of the servant of the centurion of Capernaum

What has been said about an illness manifesting in a child as an expression of the sin of the parents applied equally, at the dawn of the new era, to the relationship between master and servant. Thus in the Gospel of Matthew we hear of a centurion at Capernaum whose servant has fallen ill. While the sickness of this servant did indeed occur on the physical plane, it has huge occult significance, and was recorded in Holy Scripture for the very reason that it shows spiritual conditions in the human being in the form of a parable. This story is a typical example of the Gospels' Mystery language, which was familiar to people of those times who were rooted in ancient Hebrew culture, but which nowadays we have to decode and decipher.

First let us follow the story as it is given in Matthew:

> *And when Jesus was entered into Capernaum, there came unto him a centurion, beseeching him, And saying, Lord, my servant lieth at home sick of the palsy, grievously tormented. And Jesus saith unto him, I will come and heal him. The centurion*

answered and said, Lord, I am not worthy that thou shouldest come under my roof: but speak the word only, and my servant shall be healed. For I also am a man under authority, having soldiers under me: and I say to this man, Go, and he goeth; and to another, Come, and he cometh; and to my servant, Do this, and he doeth it. When Jesus heard it, he marvelled, and said to them that followed, Verily I say unto you, I have not found so great faith, no, not in Israel. And I say unto you, That many shall come from the east and west, and shall sit down with Abraham, and Isaac, and Jacob, in the kingdom of heaven. But the children of the kingdom shall be cast out into outer darkness: there shall be weeping and gnashing of teeth. And Jesus said unto the centurion, Go thy way; and as thou hast believed, so be it done unto thee. And his servant was healed in the selfsame hour.
(Matthew 8, 5–13)

At the beginning of Christianity, based on concepts prevalent in the ancient Jewish tradition, people still understood what was meant by the Lord healing the 'servant' of the centurion. In those times the term 'servant' signified a great deal more than it means to us today. Every letter – and thus every word still more so – concealed and contained a spiritual meaning alongside its mundane significance; and indeed, the mundane meaning was, one can say, condensed out of the meaning the word has in the spirit realm. John the Evangelist speaks of this in a still more traditional way, telling of a 'nobleman' whose 'son was sick' (John 4, 46). In those days it was understood that to say a servant or son was sick meant a sickness of the will, whereas to say a daughter was ill meant the soul was sick. We can therefore directly compare the centurion's fatally sick servant with the daughter of Jairus in relation both to the cause of illness and its healing.

This servant expresses a certain condition of the human will. At the dawn of the new era humanity was in a transitional process of separating out from itself the last echoes of the epochs of Lemuria and Atlantis. In both those epochs, human beings' life of will was focused wholly outside them. At that period the will could move objects without people needing to touch them. Later, at the time of Christ, a last echo of this could still be found, primarily amongst heathen peoples, who would 'dispatch' their will into a servant. Slavery was therefore very widespread. Judaism was

ILLNESS AND HEALING AT THE TIME OF CHRIST

somewhat more advanced, and no longer had slaves but only servants.

The centurion of Capernaum thus has a servant who does what the master wishes. The centurion's will inhabits the servant, so that when the former says: 'Do this!' he does it. But now the servant has fallen ill, and cannot do what the master says for, as we are told, he has 'the palsy' — in other words he is paralyzed.* He is incapable of acting, for the will is paralyzed. Then the centurion says: 'Lord, I am not worthy that thou shouldest come under my roof: but speak the word only, and my servant shall be healed.' This means that his roof covers and protects his house. But he is himself his house in which the will is sick. The centurion acknowledges this and asks the Christ to help him: to speak just *one* word so that his servant, his will, can recover. Through this one word the Lord will not enter physically into the centurion's house, but certainly will do so spiritually. This same process, already vouchsafed to the centurion before the Mystery of Golgotha, will come to every person on earth through the Resurrection on Easter morning. The Word that is

---

* The New International Version of the Bible in English gives the word 'paralyzed' at this point. (Translator's note.)

spoken and enters the 'house' of the centurion is the same Word celebrated in the prologue to the St John Gospel, the I AM. This I enters the habitation of the human being, enters the new house of the centurion, enlivening his sick servant — in other words healing his sick will.

The centurion recognizes Jesus of Nazareth as the Christ, the living Word of God which can heal the human being; and then he even adds: 'For I also am a man under authority, having soldiers under me.' In other words, he acknowledges that God is *his* 'centurion', just as his will must be the servant of his higher I so that it can be *divine* will. This is why John speaks of the 'nobleman', for in this sense the centurion is the servant of the true king of Israel.

We can discover how valuable these words of the centurion are when we hear Christ say: 'Verily I say unto you, I have not found so great faith, no, not in Israel.' The centurion has recognized the secret of the living Word of God which is to enter human beings.

The passage continues: 'And I say unto you, That many shall come from the east and west' — in other words from heathen lands to the East and West of Israel

— 'and shall sit down with Abraham, and Isaac, and Jacob, in the kingdom of heaven. But the children of the kingdom' — the members of the Jewish race who do not wish to acknowledge Christ but should have been able to — 'shall be cast out into outer darkness...' We can also gain a sense of the meaning of the centurion's words by considering another passage, in Mark, in which the Lord speaks to His disciples about His true mission: '...whosoever will be great among you, shall be your minister: And whosoever of you will be the chiefest, shall be servant of all. For even the Son of Man came not to be ministered unto, but to minister, and to give his life a ransom for many' (Mark 10, 43–45).

The significance of the different locations of teaching and healing

Specifically in relation to the fallen spirits Lucifer and Ahriman who manifested in illnesses at the time of Christ, there is significance in the locations where these spirits were chiefly to be found, and to which Christ went when he taught and healed.

The teachings of the Lord should be understood

literally as a process of healing, for the Word of God spoken on earth had a directly healing effect on those who had ears to hear it.

If one knows that every single word in the Gospels is precise and significant, it is possible to sense that the description of places where Christ's working was accomplished is not arbitrary or incidental, or merely insignificant embellishment.

Three kinds of locations where He worked publicly are repeatedly named in the Gospels: the temple at Jerusalem and the synagogues, in the country or mountains, and by or on the water.

I will not discuss the traditional places of teaching since most of the healings did not take place there. This was scarcely possible in the synagogues due to lack of space. (We hear of a spectacular exception to this when the bed of a paralyzed man is lowered through the roof into the inner courtyard of the synagogue at Capernaum (Mark 2, 1; Luke 9, 17). Women and children were usually not allowed to enter the synagogue or, still less so, the temple, and this applied even more strictly to non-Jews, many of whom Christ Jesus repeatedly taught and healed. In the temple and the synagogues He did not speak to the ordinary people, but there directed the Word primarily to the priests and scribes, interpreting the scriptures, explaining the words of the prophets and uttering prophecies.

But to the ordinary people who were not familiar in the same way with the extensive religious doctrines, and who most often did not even understand Hebrew – the language in which many texts of the forefathers were written – He often spoke in parables and in the open air.

Most often He taught in the country and frequently on hills – also called 'mountains' in the Gospels. In his lecture cycle on the Mark Gospel, Rudolf Steiner has already explained the significance of this term.* While it is true that the people and the group of disciples often gathered around the Redeemer on the mountains of Galilee, 'ascending the mountain' is also to be understood in supersensible terms. It meant that Christ Jesus, in ascending the Mount of Olives or Mount Tabor, could penetrate the souls of the disciples and also the ordinary people in a particularly immediate way. By ascending and spending time on a mountain, He elevated them to higher vision. The hills

---

* See Rudolf Steiner: *The Gospel of St. Mark* (op. cit.), lecture of 22 September 1912.

Christ chose for this were special locations which had already been known to the initiates of ancient times, where they had stayed or withdrawn to. The special etheric geography of these places literally made it possible to come a little closer to the world of spirit. Discovering such sacred places on earth has played a part in humanity's history for millennia – whether Egyptian, Greek or Celtic Mystery sites, or places energized by Christianity such as Mont Ségur, the hermitage in Arlesheim or the temple site in Malsch. At such places the spiritual forces, rising from the depths and entering the earth from the periphery, enable people to cultivate profound spiritual work. Even if, compared to most of the ordinary people who approached the Lord, the disciples were preordained for higher, spiritual initiation, the same step was always involved when Christ Jesus took one or several people with Him 'onto the mountain' and thus rendered them more receptive to supersensible teachings.

At these places He preached to the people in the language of ancient picture consciousness, at the same time enlivening this pictorial language, for which they had lost almost all understanding. Of course, fulfilment of the Mystery of Golgotha was necessary to lead humanity towards a new spiritual understanding and thus entirely protect them from spiritual degeneration. Yet during the brief period of Christ's life in a human body, He had to work in a different, preparatory way amongst those who encountered Him. As yet, human spirits could not be kindled by the sparks of the Whitsun spirit, which would be able to invoke a direct understanding of the Christian message irrespective of which language and culture a person was interwoven with, and where he came from. Before all this could enter the world, during the ministry of Christ in the body of Jesus of Nazareth, an interim state had to be established to make Christian teachings more accessible to the people incarnated at the time. This transitional state was in fact the re-enlivening of a certain understanding of the ancient pictorial language. The sheaths I referred to previously, from which the demons were driven out, could thus be filled and enriched with the contents of His pictorial and parable teachings in preparation for the day when the Christ spirit itself could enter and imbue them.

We can understand this spiritual situation more clearly through an example drawn from the John

Gospel. At the marriage in Cana, when Christ had only just descended into the physical body of Jesus for the first time, and the water had to be turned into wine, He said: 'Mine hour is not yet come' (John 2, 4). This hour only arrived at the Last Supper after which He no longer took this drink, and the wine became the blood of the Redeemer. Since this first Holy Communion, it is the task of the human being imbued with the blood of the Redeemer to transform the wine into water.* During the three years of Christ's work on earth, therefore, new life was breathed into the ancient picture language to preserve human beings' mind soul beyond the turning point of time, until the new bond between God and man could come into effect and the new teaching could also enter a new vessel.

The illness-inducing adversarial powers in their relationship with 'mountain' and 'water'

The Gospels describe Jesus Christ's ministry alternately on the land, i.e. on the mountain, and on or beside the water, at the same time telling us why each

---

* See Judith von Halle: *Das Abendmahl: Vom vorchristlichen Kultus zur Transubstantiation* (Verlag am Goetheanum 2006).

ILLNESS AND HEALING AT THE TIME OF CHRIST

place was chosen. At both these locations a revelation of God the Son could be given to those present in a more tangible and vivid way,* for these places were at the same time sites where the activity of the adversarial powers was revealed to the senses. The encounter between the Representative of Humanity and His fallen brothers, within sight of those who had followed Him to this place, allowed the presence of the Christ spirit within Jesus of Nazareth to manifest in a striking way specifically through the contrast with the adversarial powers appearing there.

The choice of either mountain or water as a place of teaching and healing thus lies in the connection of each with the realm of activity of the adversarial powers: to put it simply, the luciferic element was engaged on land and the ahrimanic on water.

This may initially seem contradictory, since we are likely to associate ahrimanic qualities more with land than with water. But in this domain we really should not think too associatively, which inevitably leads to

---

* See Rudolf Steiner: *The Gospel of St. Mark* (op. cit.), lecture of 22 September 1912.

misunderstandings. Instead we should carefully study the actual circumstances.

Before the Mystery of Golgotha took place, Lucifer held sway on earth. The human being's astral nature had increasingly condensed and compressed itself from the astral periphery, streaming down into the immediate vicinity of the human being's lower limbs. In this way Lucifer had also descended to the earth. The Fall from paradise was caused by the serpent, and with the human being the luciferic element also fell from the heavens down to the earth. In the Gospels we can see how, in the luciferic temptation of Christ, Lucifer tries to recreate his own fall in Christ. Everything of a degenerate astral nature now raged within and around the human being on earth. It must be emphasized that Lucifer accordingly ruled on and over the surface of the earth, not *within* the earth or beneath its surface. The interior of the earth was Ahriman's kingdom, where the latter could still unfold his forces, not yet chained by the descent of the Christ spirit into the abyss on Easter Saturday. As powerfully as Ahriman could rage in the interior of the earth — in other words pour his forces over those who penetrated the abysses of earth in death — in pre-Christian times he

ILLNESS AND HEALING AT THE TIME OF CHRIST   129

had no corresponding power over human life on earth, which instead was liable to fall prey to Lucifer. Thus, when He climbs a mountain, Christ rises to meet Lucifer. It was there that those whose souls were plagued by luciferic illnesses could more easily be healed.

> *And Jesus departed from thence, and came nigh unto the sea of Galilee; and went up into a mountain, and sat down there. And great multitudes came unto him, having with them those that were lame, blind, dumb, maimed, and many others, and cast them down at Jesus' feet* (Matthew 15, 29–30)

Lucifer's aim was to take hold of the human being who had fallen from paradise, and drag him in his piteous condition of body and soul back up to spiritual heights, away from the only place where the human being could be healed. Ahriman's aim, in contrast, was not only to gain power over death but also life, i.e. to intervene in the functions of the human body, to increasingly pour death into matter. This intention finds expression in the ahrimanic temptation of Christ, when He is urged to turn stones into bread.

The encounter with the ahrimanic being had in a

certain respect to remain superficial until the Christ passed through physical death and entered Ahriman's kingdom. These fleeting encounters took place especially during the healing of people in relation to the element of water. Ahriman worked right into this watery element – the sensory manifestation of the etheric in the physical world. While Ahriman desired to work from this element over into the solid parts of the human being – as will be shown below in a passage from the Gospels – *before* the Mystery of Golgotha he remained Lord of the underworld, which was able only to rise as far as the element of water, wherever this occurred in the material world. Thus the surface of the Sea of Galilee was a real threshold, to which Ahriman could rise from the underworld, and there enter into a certain contact also with living human beings.

The human being could allow the ahrimanic being to enter him when doubt seized hold of him about the power of the divine spirit. Such doubt existentially threatened the very fabric of his physical existence. Thus in the Matthew Gospel we hear of the encounter with water which the Lord imposed as a trial of faith on His disciples, and how, after initial faith in the power of the spirit, Peter casts doubt on this by view-

ILLNESS AND HEALING AT THE TIME OF CHRIST

ing the water and its depths in purely material terms; and at the same moment is at risk of drowning in them — in other words, in his ahrimanic view of the elements:

> *And straightway Jesus constrained his disciples to get into a ship, and to go before him unto the other side... But the ship was now in the midst of the sea, tossed with waves... And in the fourth watch of the night** [here He brings them the fourth member, the 'I', which they need in order to overcome the abyss] *Jesus went unto them, walking on the sea. And when the disciples saw him walking on the sea, they were troubled, saying, It is a spirit; and they cried out for fear. But straightway Jesus spake unto them, saying, Be of good cheer; IT IS I; be not afraid. And Peter answered him and said, Lord, if it be thou, bid me come unto thee on the water. And he said, Come. And when Peter was come down out of the ship, he walked on the water, to go to Jesus. But when he saw the wind boisterous, he was afraid; and beginning to*

---

* The fourth watch of the night corresponds to 3 a.m. The watches were divided into three-hour periods, the first beginning at six in the evening, the second at nine, and the third at midnight.

> *sink, he cried, saying, Lord, save me. And immediately Jesus stretched forth his hand, and caught him, and said unto him, O thou of little faith, wherefore didst thou doubt?...* (Matthew 14, 22–31)

In this way, prior to the Mystery of Golgotha, within the sensory manifestation of the etheric — the watery element — the ahrimanic force was able to exert power over the human being who had not yet descended into Ahriman's kingdom of death. We can recall here the ahrimanic influence in the clinical picture of the person with dropsy, which brought the fluid balance out of equilibrium and thus worked destructively on people's formative forces.

The healing of two possessed Gergesenes by the water

I would now like to look at another passage in connection with the healing of two people possessed by ahrimanic demons. This contains really very enigmatic details, but if we bring the insights of spiritual science to bear, it can clarify the relationship of Ahriman to the element of water:

ILLNESS AND HEALING AT THE TIME OF CHRIST

And when he was come to the other side into the country of the Gergesenes,* there met him two possessed with devils, coming out of the tombs, exceeding fierce, so that no man might pass by that way. And, behold, they cried out, saying, What have we to do with thee, Jesus, thou Son of God? art thou come hither to torment us before the time? And there was a good way off from them an herd of many swine feeding. So the devils besought him, saying, If thou cast us out, suffer us to go away into the herd of swine. And he said unto them, Go. And when they were come out, they went into the herd of swine: and, behold, the whole herd of swine ran violently down a steep place into the sea, and perished in the waters. And they that kept them fled, and went their ways into the city, and told every thing, and what was befallen to the possessed of the devils. And, behold, the whole city came out to meet Jesus: and when they saw him, they besought him that he would depart out of their coasts. (Matthew 8, 28–34)

---

* This is a district east of the Jordan and south-east of the Sea of Galilee.

Here too we can ascertain first of all that the demons are more perceptive than people in so far as they immediately recognize the Son of God, experiencing Him as a direct threat to their so far largely undisturbed activity. It is they who call out from the people they have possessed: 'What have we to do with thee, Jesus, thou Son of God?' Yet they add another question to their call: 'Art thou come hither to torment us before the time?' Ahriman immediately sees that Christ stands before him and, after the temptation with the stones which Christ does not turn into bread, he calculates that he will only be confronted with His manifestation and impetus when Christ — in suffering physical death — steps through the gates of his kingdom. Laying the ahrimanic being in chains, and overcoming death for all, could only be accomplished by Christ's descent into hell. The temporary expulsion of Ahriman from a few sick people's physical bodies could however already be performed 'before the time'. Ahriman naturally feels this expulsion as 'torment'.

Now, we can be somewhat surprised that the demons ask the Lord that, if they must depart from human bodies, they should be sent into a herd of pigs. However, we can discover what underlies this plea, and that it was a very cunning manoeuvre by Ahriman, through which he still hopes to triumph. What was the ahrimanic beings' idea? They hoped to insinuate themselves into human bodies before these latter descended into the underworld. The demons wished to be driven into pigs because they counted on re-entering human bodies – in multiplied fashion even – when the latter ate slaughtered pig meat, or pork. By this means they hoped to get back into human bodies.

In Judaism the consumption of pork was forbidden. It had always been regarded as not 'kosher' – from the word 'kascher' in Hebrew – and thus unclean. This uncleanness, in turn, is based on both exoteric and esoteric reasons. The exoteric reason, the details of which were certainly not known at the time, were that pork can contain so-called trichinae, or threadworms, which are not dangerous to the animal but which can cause death if introduced into the human body. We have to accentuate precisely where these ahrimanic creatures are active inside the human being: they become fatally dangerous in us the moment they infiltrate the lymph system, that is, our fluid system. In this way Ahriman would have found it easy to enter far more than just two human bodies, despite being driven out from his two first victims by the Son of God.

But his plan failed. Though Christ did send the ahrimanic demons into the herd of swine, He made sure that the animals immediately plunged over the cliffs into the water where they drowned. By this means the ahrimanic beings who had entered them were returned to the watery element and thus to Ahriman's sphere of activity below the surface of the earth and the water — from which they had first come.

The prohibition on eating unkosher meat was firmly enshrined in Jewish law. Here we can see an example of the decadence of Judaism at the dawn of the new era, noticeable in the failure to observe many old customs due to the influence of heathen tribes. The prohibition on eating pork was not just to spare people terrible pain or even death in consequence. At the time of Christ the real reason was no longer known and the custom was — if at all — only maintained out of respect for tradition. But in olden times wise people had known that eating pork allowed Ahriman entry into the human organization, and this was why the law was first ordained.

We can also find a difference between this expulsion of ahrimanic demons by Christ Jesus and the actions of the Essenes, as described by Rudolf Steiner in his lectures on the 'Fifth Gospel'. Here, reporting on his research into the Akashic Records, Steiner shows how Jesus of Nazareth, dwelling with the Essenes before the Jordan baptism, upbraided them for the way they related to demons. He even left them, in fact, due to His painful recognition of their way of life. Through special practices these Essenes kept their etheric and astral bodies largely free from the influences of the adversarial forces, but at the price of driving them out of themselves and their immediate environment into other human beings. Whenever a demon was driven out by an Essene, it migrated to another person instead, and possessed him. Christ Jesus achieved the opposite, for He did not drive the demons out of the two possessed people into the surrounding environment, but relegated them to the sphere from which they had come, thus preventing them from entering into others. The fact that the Gergesenes finally urged the Lord to leave their district, expresses the tragic aspect which the Christ impulse already bore at the dawn of the new era, and must always bear whenever it encounters evil. People had then degenerated to such an extent that they could not properly value the benefits of His deed, but, happy to violate the laws, were more interested in the profit and loss attached to their herd of swine than in their own healing and wellbeing.

The ahrimanic underworld in the Jonah story

Another passage in the Matthew Gospel also points to the sphere of Ahriman's activity below the surface of water and earth. This is when Christ disputed with the scribes about the story of the prophet Jonah:

> Then certain of the scribes and of the Pharisees answered, saying, Master, we would see a sign from thee. But he answered and said unto them, An evil and adulterous generation seeketh after a sign; and there shall no sign be given to it, but the sign of the prophet Jonas: For as Jonas was three days and three nights in the whale's belly; so shall the Son of Man be three days and three nights in the heart of the earth. The men of Nineveh shall rise in judgement with this generation, and shall condemn it: because they

repented at the preaching of Jonas; and, behold, a greater than Jonas is here. The queen of the south shall rise up in the judgement with this generation, and shall condemn it: for she came from the uttermost parts of the earth to hear the wisdom of Solomon; and, behold, a greater than Solomon is here. (Matthew 12, 38–42)

As Ahriman had previously attempted, the scribes and Pharisees now also wanted to get Jesus to perform a miracle to give proof of His divine origin. But since we should not and cannot test God, He gave them a parable-like indication of the divine impetus of His mission. And this indication was chosen specifically, for the story of Jonah gives a prophetic prefiguring of Christ's descent into the body of the earth, into the kingdom of Ahriman, when He descended to hell. And He drew the attention of the scribes and Pharisees to this story precisely because they themselves were imbued with ahrimanic characteristics, being full of doubt and hatred against the presence and reality of the Redeemer.

Jonah became a prophet because God had chosen him to proclaim His Word — not in the land of Israel but amongst the so-called heathen peoples in the great city of Nineveh. Jonah set off very reluctantly on his journey to foreign parts, lost his courage and tried to flee from the face of God, thinking he was unable to fulfil the task God had set him. As he set sail over the sea, however, the Lord unleashed a great storm. To save the ship from the threat of sinking, he ordered the sailors to throw him in the sea, for he knew that the storm was due to his disobedience. When they did this, God sent a 'great fish' (Jonah 2, 1) which swallowed him and plunged him down into the earth's etheric underworld, into which the Christ would one day descend in death. Jonah remained in the belly of this fish for 'three days and nights' and finally achieved profound faith and comfort in God, so that the Lord ordered the fish to release Jonah again. At this Jonah went to the city of Nineveh and proclaimed the Word of the Lord, at which the people professed their new faith.

Christ now reminded the Pharisees of this prophetic story, which points to the mission of the Messiah. Although they were very familiar with the writings of the prophets, they did not know the proper interpretation of the story of Jonah. The 'three days and nights' indicate the descent into the underworld and the encounter with the being of Ahriman. Although the Redeemer did not stay a full three days and nights in Ahriman's kingdom, this refers to the three Mystery days at the turning point of time: Good Friday, Easter Saturday and Easter Sunday.

But the Lord also says: *a greater than Jonas is here.* The period which Jonah spent in the underworld does not only point to Christ's descent into hell. The 'three days and nights' are more than an emblem of the Mystery of Golgotha as a unique, universal event that occurred over three days, but also stand for the future ages in the history of the world and humanity, until the end of time — until the earth has become a sun and the human being a divine creator.

The Resurrected One left His disciples a legacy of future-oriented potency in the words: 'I am with you always, even unto the end of the world' (Matthew 28, 20). In uniting with earthly nature, the Son God eternally connected Himself with this nature and with the human being — a divine deed of which neither Jonah, who spent three day and nights in the belly of the earth, nor the wise king Solomon, were capable. By transforming the earth into the body of Christ through the Mystery of Golgotha, the Son united with the earth, and would therefore remain with human beings until the end of the world. In the 'three days' we are presented with the three world days or three future planetary conditions of our earth: Jupiter, Venus and Vulcan. The 'three nights' symbolize the world nights which intervene between each of our earth's planetary embodiments: between Earth and Jupiter, Jupiter and Venus, and Venus and Vulcan, also known as the great pralayas. During these three nights too, the Christ will also be with us — since He once descended into the earth, into the realm of death — and, as leader of the Exusiai, the Spirits of Form, will ensure that the human being is able to save a renewed physical form through the world-night period and carry it over into the next planetary stage.

Both Jonah and Solomon prophetically pointed to the descent of Christ into the depths of the earth and His victory over the death of the body. Solomon built the temple — the sensory image of the divine world that was one day to become the human being's spiritual body. With his entry into the belly of the fish, Jonah accomplished the descent into Ahriman's kingdom,

ILLNESS AND HEALING AT THE TIME OF CHRIST 143

from which God saved him; for we hear him say: 'I went down to the bottoms of the mountains; the earth with her bars was about me for ever: yet hast thou brought up my life from corruption, O LORD my God' (Jonah 2, 6).

Through inner insight into this Mystery we can find one of the reasons why the Resurrected One, who appeared in the midst of the eleven disciples, was able to eat a fish: 'And as they thus spake, Jesus himself stood in the midst of them... And while they yet believed not for joy, and wondered, he said unto them, Have ye here any meat? And they gave him a piece of a broiled fish...' (Luke 24, 36–43).

As sign that He had overcome the realm of death, He ate the fish before their eyes. His physical body now encompassed the whole earth, including that watery kingdom in which Ahriman had once been active, and from which the fish came. All phenomena of the sensory world were now no longer outside but within Him, forming His body. Thus the fish which He ate was in fact not sundered from its natural element. Whereas the prophet Jonah still pointed to the Mystery of the Son, and was within the belly of the fish, the fish was now in the belly of the Son, in

Christ's earthly body. This was a sign to the disciples that Christ had truly overcome death and had risen again.

And in the words which the Master directed to the scribes, 'An evil and adulterous generation', we again find an indication of the sad fact that 'A prophet is not without honour, save in his own country...' (Matthew 13, 57). The prophecies of Jonah and Solomon were, after all, to be fulfilled in Him. But they were not ready to believe it. Thus Christ bemoans the fact that even the heathen people of Nineveh accepted what Jonah proclaimed, but here is one greater than Jonah. And the Queen of Sheba – likewise a heathen – accepted the wisdom of Solomon; but here is one greater than Solomon. For what stood in their midst, amongst this prepared and chosen race of the priests of Israel, was the living Word of God; and they did not wish to accept this Word. The once heathen people of Nineveh and the Queen of Sheba therefore proved better in the eyes of heaven than the race of priests and scribes of the chosen people who, instead of renewing their bond with God, were in the process of rupturing it.

Thus the story of the healing of the possessed Gergesenes and the instruction in the secret of the Jonah story which Christ gave the Pharisees shows us how the ahrimanic quality was revealed from the depths of the earth through the watery element in the pre-Christian world of matter, where it could ultimately lead to physical illnesses such as dropsy or 'possession by devils' (Matthew 8, 28) — as possession of the etheric body.

Illnesses Today

The nature of illnesses today

An example from the Gospels can easily show how the underlying causes of illness have changed markedly through the ages:

> *After this there was a feast of the Jews; and Jesus went up to Jerusalem. Now there is at Jerusalem by the sheep market a pool, which is called in the Hebrew tongue Bethesda, having five porches. In these lay a great multitude of impotent folk, of blind, halt, withered, waiting for the moving of the water. For an angel went down at a certain season into the pool, and troubled the water: whosoever then first after the troubling of the water stepped in was made whole of whatsoever disease he had...* (John 5, 1–4)

At the time of Christ there were two such healing pools in Jerusalem: one in the north-east of the city, directly adjoining the so-called sheep's gate, through which traders from other parts drove their animals to market at the nearby forum. This was the pool of Bethesda. The second was in the south-east of the city, by the Hinnom valley, and was called the pool of Siloah. The pool of Bethesda in particular was thought to have healing properties, resulting from the occurrences which the John Gospel reports.

Hundreds of sick people gathered both by and in the pool of Bethesda every day; but animals which were to be slaughtered as offerings in the temples, or sold at the market, were also cleaned in the waters of the pool. Healthy people also went into the pool to wash, bathe their children and even to get drinking water.

It is not necessary to have witnessed events at the turning point of time to realize the dire hygienic state the pool water must have been in, even if it was renewed occasionally by a stream that flowed into it whenever a thermal spring north of the city surged more strongly.

But this passage shows us that understanding of water's source and quality has completely changed two thousand years after the pool was used as described in the Gospels. In those times water was not regarded as intrinsically fresh or renewed because a thermal source occasionally fed into it. The unpredictable pulsation of the water was ascribed to the movements of an angel, and we have to admit that this interpretation is certainly as true as the explanation just given. In reality we have here two views which do not conflict: an esoteric and exoteric one. We do not have to deny the impetus of a spiritual power when we see the sudden pulsation of the source as reason for the water's movement. On the contrary, the impetus of divine spiritual forces in the earth body doubtless precedes, as their real cause, the natural effects perceptible with our outer senses. Thus how we view the origin and also the quality of water depends on our spiritual outlook.

Accordingly, only an overly intellectual and materialistic view of the conditions of the time will find it surprising that people did not fall ill when they bathed in this pool or drank its water. Ingrained or dyed-in-the-wool orthodox physicians and microbiologists will naturally assert that it can no longer be proven today how many people ultimately died from contact with this water. But we should not make the common assumption that people at the time of Christ had no gift for observation or healthy human reason. People then

ILLNESSES TODAY

were certainly not so stupid that they would embark on pilgrimages in their thousands to these pools if this caused them lasting harm. On the contrary, we hear that these pools were well known for their healing properties. But how could this healing effect arise? People's belief in the reality of the spiritual world made it possible. And I want to emphasize here that this does not refer to the power of suggestion — also often nowadays dismissed as superstition — but that this involved faith in the *reality* of spiritual forces, the acknowledgement of the source of all substance in the supersensible.

People sensitively perceived the spirit in the water, and as long as they drank, as it were, the spirit with the water, any impurities in it could not harm them, but instead their drink even exerted a healing effect. A health-threatening microbial pollutant only enters water when it is de-spiritualized or sundered from spirit.

We ourselves create our own conditions of life. If we do not recognize the spiritual reality in water, bacteria and other microbes can settle in it, and then the same water which once had healing properties becomes a life-threatening breeding ground for illnesses.

It would certainly be a fatal error to think that we could drink from a comparable 'muck-pond' today without suffering harmful consequences, 'simply' by believing in the spirit in water. In an age when the most varied pathogens, such as coli bacteria, have been thoroughly researched and enumerated, it would be mere naivety to think that we could drink from such water if we tell ourselves that the good spirit is active in it. Of course we will fall ill if we drink such water.

Here the whole situation is reversed and it becomes apparent that today we must *inevitably* fall ill from impure water *because* we know that it is polluted with microbes. It doesn't even matter whether or not the person who drinks the water himself knows this, for knowledge of microbes is now present in the world. Humanity as a whole has developed knowledge in the domain of microbiology, discovering, observing and describing the germs it sought under the microscope. In the history of medicine in the modern age, it was not a question of some devastating bacterial illness suddenly appearing out of the blue, leading people to seek the supposed microbiological triggers. The appearance of a disease such as Spanish flu (alongside other

ILLNESSES TODAY

pathogens) was, if we observe this carefully, preceded and dependent upon ideas people developed about dangerous micro-organisms. Once a thought or concept is formulated for the first time in humanity, this is then followed by the outbreak of the corresponding illness, and subsequently people seek and actually find the cause. But the first stage was the idea of finding something like bacteria or viruses, and the second the discovery of the pathogen itself. Now, therefore, these bacteria are as active and real in the physical world as the good angel in the water at the dawn of the new era.

Thus we can now reverse the question as to how the water's healing effect could act: How could the originally healing effect of the water be lost, and be replaced by a harmful effect?

By developing a different kind of thinking through the centuries, and a different view of the world and the spiritual beings at work in it, humanity itself changed the conditions governing its sphere of life. Especially since the beginning of the consciousness soul age, illnesses have altered. This is not only connected with the fact that Christ has become the Lord of Karma since the Mystery of Golgotha, and that outbreaks of illness now therefore occur in a subsequent incarnation and not — as in pre-Christian times — in the same incarnation in which the predisposition for an illness was laid down. This fact alone would only alter the perspective on the karma of illness extending, since then, across several lives, without affecting the nature and types of illness. Today, though, different clinical pictures occupy the foreground of medicine. Paralysis, blindness, deafness or muteness today account for a far smaller percentage of disorders than they did at the time of Christ. In their place have come ever more of the so-called infectious diseases. As humanity advanced further in the scientific field, and discovered micro-organisms such as bacteria and viruses, these began to take on ever more virulent forms. Only then did the activity and significance of, for instance, bacteria, assume highly dangerous proportions. The more that human beings ascribed importance to *matter* rather than to spirit, the more they created the preconditions for bacteria and viruses to exist. By saying this I do not mean to question scientific advances, or label them as negative. This simply shows that as scientific knowledge increases, so does the strength of the opponent against which one is fighting.

ILLNESSES TODAY

At the dawn of the new era, the laborious procedures now compulsory amongst medical staff, such as disinfecting hands or sterilizing surgical tools, would simply not have been necessary — for one reason because the invasive or extensive medical interventions which now happen on a daily basis were scarcely known. The illnesses prevalent at the time did not necessitate such interventions. And if these interventions existed, as in ancient Egyptian culture, they did not require today's 'germ-free' conditions, but were magical acts carried out by priests, since the human being was then still seen for what he is: an image of the gods; and not an image of the ape, diverging from the latter only by a few gene sequences.

Over many years, Rudolf Steiner repeatedly pointed out that scientific engagement with the human being and nature must once more become a pursuit imbued with ethics and morality:

> *Our civilization can never progress if the laboratory table does not become a kind of altar, if synthesis and analysis do not become a kind of spiritual art, and people do not become aware that they are*

intervening in world evolution by doing one thing or another.*

Likewise, the following remark by Rudolf Steiner can strike us as an earnest warning when we think of current stem cell and genetic research, though such warnings seem to go largely unheard in the circles where this work is done:

All re-creation and representation of living things will only be permissible for us if this is performed in so earnest and pure a way that the laboratory table becomes our altar... People today will never be able to re-create and represent anything drawn from living nature without the help of beings who stand behind nature, and so long as this does not become a sacramental act for us.†

We may scarcely wish to contemplate what it means that 'living nature' is indeed nowadays already being 're-created and represented' in laboratories, but cer-

---

* See Rudolf Steiner: *Natur und Geistwesen – ihr Wirken in unserer sichtbaren Welt* (GA 98), lecture of 26 June 1921.
† See Rudolf Steiner: *Esoteric Lessons 1904–1914* (SteinerBooks 2007), lecture of 5 December 1907.

ILLNESSES TODAY

tainly not under those sacramental conditions which Rudolf Steiner saw as necessary for our civilization's progress.

We ought therefore to return to the stance towards the mysteries of life at work within us which we once had in the times of the ancient Mysteries. But we also need to draw this stance from a unifying insight that is not in conflict either with our scientific advances nor our spiritual evolution, that is, our spiritual-scientific research. Since the advent of the consciousness soul age, the words of Christ on the Cross — 'Father, forgive them; for they know not what they do' (Luke 23, 34) — hold true only to a very limited degree. Today humanity can know what it is doing, and it even has the duty to know it. Christ's loving deed of sacrifice gave us the freedom and opportunity to find our own way, voluntarily, to the spirit, and not to be tied to it, as it were, by an umbilical cord. This is the prerequisite for humans to become divine. This freedom was linked with I-consciousness, for only thereby can it be grasped. I-consciousness, in turn, places us in a position of responsibility towards our own actions, and thus we must account for everything which we bring about in the course of earth's evolution.

The causes of modern illnesses

Today, likewise, illnesses are caused by the conditions and circumstances which human beings themselves create: not just our actions but also our feelings and thoughts. The nature of all illnesses that have ever appeared on earth is directly connected with the human being's evolution. Illnesses were, are and will continue to be the sensory expression of each person's state of soul and spirit. But since the beginning of the age of the consciousness soul, they are also increasingly becoming an expression of the soul-spiritual state of the whole human race. After the Mystery of Golgotha was accomplished and the consciousness soul awoke, humanity has increasingly needed to develop a concept of sickness and health that is different from the pre-Christian one, and that has a fraternal and holistic quality. Based on the uniting impetus of Christ's loving sacrifice, humanity needs to see itself as a social organism

ILLNESSES TODAY

which can fall ill just as much as the individual standing within it.

We have to regard it as a tragic fate but at the same time as evidence and illustration of the context described here that the Spanish flu referred to above broke over humanity like a scourge during the First World War — at a time therefore when huge losses of human life were already being inflicted. At this time, scientific advances had not only brought new developments in scientific medicine but also in the field of technology and thus in the domain of warfare. Machine guns and nerve gas are just two of the countless inventions of the modern age — since the fall of the spirits of darkness in 1879 — which human beings used in a bestial way to rob their brothers of health and life. All this ensued from the dishonest politics of the time, from delusional ideas about nations and races, law and history. The beast that humanity created at this time in its thinking and emotions finally took a form corresponding to such thinking and emotions as countless millions of viruses.

Through his occult research, Rudolf Steiner established a connection between the dark power which today already looks forward to the 'black age' of Orifiel and the bacilli which 'devour and spoil human physical bodies'. He states that the preconditions for the outbreak of 'dire illnesses and plagues' are created by 'fraternal strife and internecine war' — in other words the sickness of the social organism. Establishing this connection between the workings of dark powers amongst nations and also individuals, and the outbreak of infectious diseases which 'attack poor human bodies' and leave them to 'waste away', gives shocking insight into the current state of the modern world. Such plagues, against which scarcely any medicines have yet proved effective, are already afflicting us, long before the advent of the age of Orifiel around 2400 AD.

In the same esoteric lesson given on 5 December 1907 — i.e. long before the First World War had started — Rudolf Steiner made a connection between the formation of 'bacilli' and the god Mammon.* Mammon is the prevailing anti-spirit of our age who opposes the time spirit Michael. Whereas Michael, the good time spirit and serving helper of Christ, has largely been abandoned by humanity as he tries to lead us towards

---

* Ibid., lecture of 5 December 1907.

a healthy social form along the lines of the threefold social organism, human beings instead render homage to Mammon. If human beings hearkened to Michael they would 'actively take up ... Michael's wise direction',* and also allow the workings of the spirits of personality to unfold in them, leading to a panoramic vision of history and the ability to rightly perceive and connect karmic facts of life and individual circumstances.

In relation to illnesses Rudolf Steiner's statement about the connection between the rise of bacilli and the appearance of the god Mammon is proving accurate. No one today, at least, will doubt the link between Mammon and the commercial position of chemical and pharmaceutical companies in western society, which benefit financially from the ever-increasing outbreaks of epidemics. Humanity's way of thinking has become so corrupt that it can no longer even realize how absurd it is that production of medicines is subject to financial interests — for instance that the treatment of millions of people with AIDS is, in all

---

*See Rudolf Steiner: *Breathing the Spirit* (Rudolf Steiner Press 2002).

seriousness, dependent on the activities of profit-oriented stock market speculators.

The arrival of new diseases that have not yet been wholly explained and for which no remedy has yet been found, is also connected with the appearance of that third, dark power which stands in complete opposition to Christianity and thus also to the Christian impulse for healing. With the end of the twentieth century — for the third time since the Mystery of Golgotha — it is mustering its forces against humanity's spiritual awakening.

Humanity, which is developing in the course of its evolution towards an ever more common, general clairvoyance, is hindered by this anti-Christian impulse from putting this clairvoyance to healthy use, and thereby progressing towards spiritual knowledge. It is certainly regrettable that a considerable part of medical and pharmacological knowledge is falling under the sway of these tendencies.

If we look more carefully at so-called Attention Deficit Disorder, we will find that treating even young children with long-term administration of tranquillizers

ILLNESSES TODAY

serves to cover up and deaden subtle signs of the perception of spiritual worlds, which the majority of parents regard as alien or 'abnormal', instead of channelling and cultivating these in a way that would enhance the child's wellbeing. Modern educational approaches are a fundamental problem. If a child expresses something that he experiences within himself as true, but then finds no response from his parent or teacher, or even meets with disapproval, a great conflict will be kindled between the generations. Such conflict is however still the expression of a healthy process; but if it is impressed on a child at the very earliest stage that what he experiences and says is mistaken and morbid, the situation will increasingly get out of control. In relation to education, therefore, it is really hardly a matter of asking how we should discipline our children or how we should treat an increasing number of 'sick' children, but of asking instead what the educator can bring to the child, and whether he is attentive to the changes occurring in the human being and humanity as a whole. Those unaware of the overall context cannot grasp what harm will be done to humanity in future by administering chemical sedatives and thus implanting something into many souls of a whole generation. This is in complete opposition to what had begun to germinate in these souls, that should have been cared for and cultivated as precious spiritual possession. Giving such sedatives aims ultimately to suppress our awareness of the plan of Ahriman and Sorat, which is to stand the world on its head yet at the same time give us the illusory sense that things are how they should be, so as to harness us to their service.

As long ago as 1917, Rudolf Steiner pointed to a corresponding tendency in human evolution:

> *And the time will come ... when people will say that for human beings to think of spirit and soul is itself sick, and the only people who are healthy are those who talk of the body and nothing else. People will regard it as a symptom of illness if someone develops in such a way that he forms the idea that there is such a thing as spirit or soul. Such people will be regarded as sick. And – you can be quite sure of this – a corresponding medicine will be found to counteract this.*
>
> *At that time [The Council of Constantinople], the spirit was abolished. The soul will likewise be*

> *abolished by medicine. Based on a 'healthy outlook' people will find a vaccine which will manipulate the organism, where possible in the earliest infancy, even at birth, in such a way that this human body cannot arrive at the idea that a soul and spirit exist. That is how sharply opposed the two world views will become.**

The global trade in sleeping tablets and other sedatives is now flourishing as never before. Humanity cannot sleep peacefully because, in its higher I, it cannot — despite everything — reconcile the active spiritual realities with its often diametrically opposed world view and corresponding mode of life. We are being inundated from without by substances that push far beyond our reach the capacity to become aware of spiritual processes. The fact that the god Mammon has a tight grasp on the pharmaceutical companies responsible for producing these substances is one of the bitter facts of life that scarcely anyone now questions.

---

* See Rudolf Steiner: *The Fall of the Spirits of Darkness* (Rudolf Steiner Press 2008), lecture of 7 October 1917.

The nature of 'non-karmic illnesses'

Evident lack of knowledge about the spiritual roots and causes of our illnesses means that a significant section of mainstream medicine is today — certainly involuntarily — going headlong towards transforming the Christian impulse of healing into its opposite. Various studies have been undertaken in recent years on the dire and almost countless side effects arising either directly or in the medium term from intake of chemical drugs. Despite this, the use of antibiotics to treat infectious diseases, or chemotherapy to treat cancer, are still regarded as almost sacred and indisputable ways to tackle disease. Serious alternatives have not so far really been forthcoming either, since for this to happen our whole concept of the human being would have to change fundamentally.

It is now conceivable therefore that illness, which was once a gift of the good gods with a view to providing karmic compensation, or as a help for our spiritual progress, can no longer come to full fruition, and therefore may be carried over into a subsequent life, perhaps in an aggravated form.

In this context we should also take a closer look at

ILLNESSES TODAY

what are now controversial vaccination policies. There is only space to just touch here on what happens, from a spiritual perspective, when a child is vaccinated. A germ of the illness that is to be combated is injected into the human body, with the aim of teaching the child's organism to self-immunize. And yet a defenceless child must then continue to bear this illness within himself. Thus something is implanted into an individual which comes from without and might never otherwise have entered him. The basic idea of vaccination is of course not intrinsically wrong, corresponding as it does to the homeopathic principle of treating like with like. Yet the way in which this is practised today — i.e. not after an illness has arisen, as in homeopathy, but prior to it ever breaking out, so that we cannot even really talk of 'therapy' — takes no account of the spiritual background to illness in each individual. Thus a child today can be faced with a destiny that does not belong to him at all — either through having an illness implanted in him that karma would never otherwise have brought him into contact with; or through the fact that immunization prevents his destiny from an experience of the illness karma would have given him, since this illness cannot fully develop. It must therefore be carried over for a future life, in which quite other things ought really to occur due to new conditions brought about by the current life.

Since a great part of western medicine overlooks the soul-spiritual causes of karmic illnesses, focusing instead solely on their material symptoms, material means are also used to combat them which one cannot in fact really call 'medicines'. The appearance of an illness is perceived on or in the body, then diagnosed and treated physically by material means. By doing this, however, one doubles the 'wrongness': what I mean by this is that one does not just overlook the spiritual causes and therefore treat only material symptoms, but also that these external effects are not treated with medicines derived from spiritual insight, but from purely material perspectives.

The doctor therefore introduces something into the patient from without and treats him from one aspect only, which has nothing at all to do with the spiritual and karmic cause.

If he prescribes an antibiotic, the name itself can tell us what will occur in the patient's organism: 'anti-bios' means 'against life'. Such a medicine not only kills the

ILLNESSES TODAY

pathogen it is directed at, but *before* this usually recalcitrant and often also quickly resistant invader, also all other 'life' in the human organism, in particular what is nowadays called the 'immune system'.

I have suggested that humanity's impoverished conceptual life, which does not correspond to spiritual realities, may be responsible for the rise of new illnesses. The AIDS illness already mentioned is, basically, one example of a contagion of the spirit. Only relatively recently did human beings develop the idea that we descend from apes. It is only a few decades since the theory derived from Darwin, that human beings have animal ancestors, found its way into school books and thus into society in general. Within a very short period, therefore, we relinquished the view of ourselves – that we came from the lap of the gods – which had always previously existed in our inner life, ever since physical human beings entered into the material world. Today the majority of people in the so-called civilized world now deny their divine nature, and in doing so distance themselves not only in a more spiritual sense from their true humanity but also certainly in a physical sense too. Since this Darwinian idea has taken effect we have had a reflection of it in the external physical world, in the human immunodeficiency virus (HIV). This was present in apes,* and may even have lived in them for millennia. But only in the past 40 years has it become deadly to human beings. Since the human being started to see his own origins in his genetic connection with the great ape, he has fallen ill from a pathogen that lives in this creature. He is thus dying from his own 'fixed' idea — from an anti-Christian concept of human existence.†

Here the impure thing in the human being is not really the HIV itself but the concept he has formed of himself.

In the Matthew Gospel we find an account of Christ Jesus's teachings about what really pollutes the human being and what does not:

> *And he called the multitude, and said unto them, Hear, and understand: Not that which goeth into the mouth defileth a man; but that which cometh out of the mouth, this defileth a man. Then came his dis-*

---

* See article 'Das Virus das aus der Wärme kam — Wie der AIDS-Erreger die Welt eroberte', *Basler Zeitung*, 2 November 2007.

† Also referred to by Peter Tradowsky, New Year lecture 2002, private printing (Berlin 2003).

> *ciples, and said unto him, Knowest thou that the Pharisees were offended, after they heard this saying? But he answered and said, Every plant, which my heavenly Father hath not planted, shall be rooted up. Let them alone: they be blind leaders of the blind. And if the blind lead the blind, both shall fall into the ditch. Then answered Peter and said unto him, Declare unto us this parable. And Jesus said, Are ye also yet without understanding? Do not ye yet understand, that whatsoever entereth in at the mouth goeth into the belly, and is cast out into the draught? But those things which proceed out of the mouth come forth from the heart; and they defile the man. For out of the heart proceed evil thoughts, murders, adulteries, fornications, thefts, false witness, blasphemies: These are the things which defile a man: but to eat with unwashen hands defileth not a man.* (Matthew 15, 10–20)

The AIDS illness and also other epidemics breaking over humanity today should be seen in a different light from those illnesses which, as karmic destiny, connect each individual with his soul-spiritual development and are sent us as aid in this development by the good spirits.

We can certainly say that something new has entered the history of humanity's illnesses over recent decades: the outbreak of 'non-karmic' illnesses. This concept is not entirely accurate though, for these illnesses too are karmic in nature, though not in relation to the individual. The phrase however indicates a particular development, differentiating those illnesses which lie in an individual's karmic destiny from those which we can contract although they do *not* form part of our karmic path. These new illnesses, to which we can succumb, are triggered by the sick social organism.

It is characteristic of the 'non-karmic' illnesses that one cannot find any karmic 'debt' to explain the outbreak of such an illness in the destiny of the individual concerned. What human beings bring into the world in the form of anti-Christian thinking, feeling and will, instead of preparing to perceive the etheric Christ, floods the world with demonic forces. The physical and sensory manifestations of these demons are the phenomena of illness which human beings cannot explain by purely scientific means. These include not only infectious diseases but also what must be called the real cultural epidemic of dementia and Alzheimer's, which are spreading increasingly in the western world,* as well as the so-called auto-immune diseases such as lupus and multiple sclerosis. All these epidemic-type diseases are characterized by the fact that, as signs of an anti-Christian impetus, they attack people who do not have the corresponding karmic predisposition to them.

With the rise of such epidemics the organism of humanity is showing the same reaction to poor treatment as the earth organism does to the treatment which it receives. As reaction to the general deeds of humanity, the organism of humanity throws up epidemics, while the earth organism is rent with earthquakes and volcanic eruptions. Those who have not themselves caused the harm are usually in fact the ones who suffer most.

Once again in human history, therefore, some illnesses are today not being caused by the good gods but by the activity of evil forces. But at the time of Christ, when this state of affairs was still justified, Lucifer and Ahriman were responsible for the

---

* A study on this theme by Judith von Halle is due to be published in German in 2008.

appearance of an illness, whereas today the third power that opposes the Christ impulse is at work, and uses Lucifer and Ahriman as its servants to realize its plan.

When Lucifer and Ahriman unfolded their effects at the time of Christ, this involved a weakening of the human astral and etheric bodies as cause of a particular physical disorder. In the modern illnesses referred to above, however, the cause is a weakening of the highest of the four sheaths or bodies of the human being, the I.

When the gift of Christ, the I, is weakened or sick, the attacking forces can only be called luciferic or ahrimanic in so far as they serve the third, dark, anti-Christian power. Rudolf Steiner spoke of this power, which he said would in future afflict humanity like a plague, as the 'Sorat Mystery'.* The peculiarity of such illnesses consists, as we have already seen, in the fact that these powers do not necessarily impact on the I that has become weak. The nature of these disorders can therefore point us to the egotistic rather than I-oriented condition of the human social context.

---

* See Rudolf Steiner: *Book of Revelation* (Rudolf Steiner Press 1998), lecture of 10 June 1915.

ILLNESSES TODAY

Humanity can also fall sick in its group or humanity I, if it lapses from its connection with the Christ being, within which it could stand today.

The spiritual task of Europe consists in mediating between impulses from East and West. While the East is subject to a luciferic influence, the ahrimanic comes to expression more in the West. Between human striving away from the earth, towards 'Nirvana' — a visionary but I-less concept of karma — on the one hand, and the abolition of soul and spirit through worship of matter alone on the other, a force of the Centre needs to be active. This is depicted in Steiner's sculptural group, in which the Representative of Humanity brings together the extremes of duality into a balanced and healing trinity.*

The illnesses with which people increasingly have to battle today, which are *not* karmic in nature, are directly linked with the sickness of the social organism. For Europeans this means that they are connected with the unachieved moral, spiritual and Christian aims of his culture. Europe is increasingly falling under the sway of primarily Anglo-American impulses,

---

* See Rudolf Steiner: *Destinies of Individuals and Nations* (Rudolf Steiner Press 1986), lecture of 10 June 1915.

instead of bearing into the western world the balancing element of the Christian centre. To the extent that this occurs, Europeans are contracting the 'cultural illnesses' of the western world.

This anti-Christian trait in the social organism can only be brought back into equilibrium by innocent people having in a certain sense — with Christ as exemplar — to give up their health and life for that of the perpetrators. This will continue until humanity eventually learns, bitterly, that it is a single organism, and that through chauvinistic nationalism or economic disparity it differentiates itself into either less or more advantaged social groups or nations, and in doing so cuts off its own limbs, like arms and legs. Then we will realize that our thinking and actions have inevitably impacted on the *overall* social organism. Only when understanding for the new I-endowed group soul consciousness matures within humanity, and when those who have been sick in their hearts yet not in their bodies take full, spiritual responsibility for their actions so as to rid the world of those illnesses, will it be possible to halt the outbreak of new epidemics.

The process of growing more aware of the reality of the world of spirit and thus of the significance of the healing impulses which Christ brought into the physical world therefore contains inexhaustible potential, particularly in relation to the treatment of already existing karmic and non-karmic illnesses, and the prevention of new ones.

The Future Impulse of Healing

The Christian impulse of healing today and in the future

An illness, understandably, is usually felt by the person concerned and also by his family as a terrible misfortune. No one who falls ill is likely to be pleased about it. Yet we can observe that children especially — who, because they have spent only a short while on the physical earth, usually have a closer connection with the world of spirit than adults — cope better with a severe illness than their relatives who are not directly affected. Those who fall ill quite often develop a sense that their illness is due to fulfilment of a higher purpose which they themselves may not understand but whose meaning they increasingly recognize and value. In our civilization today, the great, beneficent spiritual forces which an illness can bring to light in the human being are often suppressed or overlooked, since people regard the material body as the highest human possession, and its decline or decay as the tragic end of a human existence.

THE FUTURE IMPULSE OF HEALING

But all that we need to bring before our soul in illness and in the face of death, so that we can gain useful benefit from our destiny, is Christ's journey through the earthly vale of pain into the heavenly kingdom of God. *He* is our Representative of Humanity. *He* pointed the way for us through suffering, through the all-embracing task of personal will to rebirth in a true, life-giving human existence.

The healings accomplished at the turning point of time have been passed down to us in the Gospels, and by certain souls whose spiritual vision was able to bear witness to them. These healings can be a help to us in understanding the Christian impulse of healing in the present and the future. Even though the illnesses of those times and the course they took were different from today, they could only be healed through the Christ impulse, just as is the case in the present era.

At that time the Christ impulse worked for three years, between the Jordan baptism and the Resurrection, in the human being Jesus of Nazareth, and was given to sick souls from without. Today it works in each one of us and, with sufficient devotion and care, can provide the forces from within that make healing possible. Such healing can initially only refer to healing of the soul. Healing of the body will likewise come about through the Christ forces within people over future centuries and millennia. As the human being's material body gradually degenerates, this healing will, at the same time, come about through the ongoing development of our spirit body – which Rudolf Steiner designates the 'resurrection body' – in imitation of Christ as our exemplar.

If we penetrate this with our thinking, we can conclude that once this resurrection body has been fully and thoroughly formed, the purpose and effect of karma as it exists today for the human being will have changed. We can imagine this path of evolution in reverse: someone who has developed his resurrection body – i.e. his spiritualized physical body – towards the end of the planetary embodiment of Earth, can no longer suffer illness in his old material body, for he has been able to discard it like an old, empty skin. If he can no longer suffer illness in this material body, karmic illness can no longer play a part for him. If, in turn, there is no karmic illness any longer, this means that the human being develops further in his soul in such a way that he no longer gives rise to any further illness.

THE FUTURE IMPULSE OF HEALING

This soul evolution, and thus the preservation of health, is something we only acquire through the power of the I. The I will then have become so mature and strong in us that it will act as continual guardian over our bodily sheaths — in the same way that the I of the I-bringer Jesus Christ acted as guardian for the lower bodily sheaths of people at the dawn of the new era. When He endowed them with the forces of His I, the demons were driven out of their bodily sheaths, and illness departed from their body.

In this way, the I and bodily nature, the Christ impulse and the healing of the body, are connected with each other.

In future, therefore, our concept of karma will undergo a transformation to the degree that we change our soul-spiritual and thus also physical condition. The basis of the karma concept of the distant future — which will apply to the earth's next planetary stage of embodiment — can today already be conceived and understood by observing and cultivating three qualities which are inherent in Christ: love, compassion and conscience.

The new karma of the Jupiter earth will form from

internalizing these three cornerstones of the Christian spirit in thought and feeling, and from will-penetrated realization of them. In those far-distant times, mature souls who no longer suffer physical illness, as described above, will unite in full consciousness with the destiny of another soul in need of help, i.e. with their karma. These mature souls will devote themselves, in love, compassion and conscience, to taking on the karma of illness of other souls, whose 'I's are so weak or wasted that they are unable to help themselves. Thus an I-permeated, helping soul of the future will take on the karma of illness of another human being, and will bear it in his place so that he can regain health. Through such a deed of sacrifice the – in a Christian sense – advanced or developed human being will on Jupiter increasingly come to resemble Christ.

Today we can already make this evolution on the distant Jupiter earth understandable and even actively prepare for it through awareness of the importance of the human sense of ego or I, which Rudolf Steiner recognized as the twelfth sense in modern human beings. This I sense is distinguished by the fact that it

THE FUTURE IMPULSE OF HEALING

does not — or not only — relate to grasping our *own* I, but rather that of the *other*. As such the I sense is the highest of all human senses and today already forms a preparatory stage and foundation for what will constitute the spiritualized human being of the future, and develop him into a self-sacrificing, helping soul. Thus the I sense can even be said to give a foretaste of our future human existence. Today, as highest of the upper senses, it is already present in us as a future constituent of the spiritualized human organism of Vulcan earth, where it will form the lowest and thus foundational sense for grasping and penetrating the world of spirit.

For our immediate present, and for future decades and centuries, this evolution will be initiated as we increasingly learn to find our own salvation in supporting the other. If someone falls ill today, the mission of the karmic illness means that the idea of karma can more easily kindle in him, and thus his I is supported in awakening into spirit consciousness. But something quite particular occurs which leads towards the future evolution described above: not only does our illness usually lead us on a wholly new path and potentially to a new impetus in our lives, but it also offers others the opportunity to awaken to Christian feeling and deed.

Our illness is therefore at the same time a wakening call to the compassion of the other. Only when we can feel compassion with the other's destiny – in this case in the form of illness – can we also develop the active power to heal.

Thus medicine, in so far as it really serves the impulse of healing, is based entirely on loving interest, on the healthy person's compassion for the destiny of the sick person. The impulses which the healthy person here expends and gives out, are archetypally Christian. Even if a person cannot directly offer specialist medical help, and is therefore not able to concern himself with specific, physical matters, his interest and involvement will exert a healing effect on the patient. Through soulfully suffering with the other (the literal meaning of 'com-passion'), he helps the other more quickly realize his karma.

In addition, with every motion of his sympathy he powerfully counteracts the destructive impulses of the future, which Rudolf Steiner spoke of in relation to the annulment of the soul. Whoever can feel sympathy and compassion will not allow his soul's existence to be denied him, and nor, therefore, the existence of a world in which this is rooted.

In the sculptural group in Dornach, the Representative of Humanity stands in the centre. Rudolf Steiner wanted to show the three cornerstones of the Christian spirit — love, compassion and conscience — shining forth from the sculptured form of His countenance. This is how it appeared to his inner eye already in May 1912, two years before he made the first actual drafts for the 'Group', when he spoke in Cologne about the figure of the Representative of Humanity as follows:

> *Compassion and love are the forces from which Christ forms His etheric body through to the end of earth evolution... From the impulses of conscience of individual human beings, Christ draws His physical body.**

At the same time as these features slowly began to take shape in the artistic depiction of the Christ countenance in the sculpture studio in Dornach, Rudolf

---

* See Rudolf Steiner: *Erfahrungen des Übersinnlichen. Die drei Wege der Seele zu Christus* (GA 143), lecture of 8 May 1912.

Steiner first gave the so-called Samaritan verse to members from Berlin at the outbreak of the First World War:

> *As long as you experience the pain*
> *Which leaves me unscathed*
> *Christ working in world being*
> *Is unperceived.*
> *For weak the spirit remains*
> *When, alone in its own body*
> *It stays immune from feeling suffering.*
>
> *So lang du den Schmerz erfühlest*
> *Der mich meidet,*
> *Ist Christus unerkannt*
> *Im Weltenwesen wirkend.*
> *Denn schwach nur bleibt der Geist*
> *Wenn er allein im eignen Leibe*
> *Des Leidesfühlens mächtig ist.**

We find the parable of the merciful Samaritan in the words of the Evangelist and physician Luke, which I would like to recall here:

---

* See Rudolf Steiner: *Destinies of Individuals and Nations* (op. cit.), lecture of 1 September 1914.

And, behold, a certain lawyer stood up, and tempted him, saying, Master, what shall I do to inherit eternal life? He said unto him, What is written in the law? how readest thou? And he answering said, Thou shalt love the Lord thy God with all thy heart, and with all thy soul, and with all thy strength, and with all thy mind; and thy neighbour as thyself. And he said unto him, Thou hast answered right: this do, and thou shalt live. But he, willing to justify himself, said unto Jesus, And who is my neighbour? And Jesus answering said, A certain man went down from Jerusalem to Jericho, and fell among thieves, which stripped him of his raiment, and wounded him, and departed, leaving him half dead. And by chance there came down a certain priest that way: and when he saw him, he passed by on the other side. And likewise a Levite, when he was at the place, came and looked on him, and passed by on the other side. But a certain Samaritan, as he journeyed, came where he was: and when he saw him, he had compassion on him, And went to him, and bound up his wounds, pouring in oil and wine, and set him on his own beast, and brought him to an inn, and took care of him. And on the morrow when he departed, he took out two pence, and gave them to the host, and said unto him, Take care of him; and whatsoever thou spendest more, when I come again, I will repay thee. Which now of these three, thinkest thou, was neighbour unto him that fell among the thieves? And he said, He that shewed mercy on him. Then said Jesus unto him, Go, and do thou likewise. (Luke 10, 25–37)

This parable of mercy leads us to Rudolf Steiner's Samaritan verse, which embodies those three prime Christian qualities, love, compassion and conscience. 'Experience' of the other is an expression of the capacity to love. It is not just feeling, a cautious sensing, but an active turning towards the being of another. 'Experiencing' the other is the *love* which proceeds from one's own I. In 'feeling suffering' is expressed our involvement in the pain of another, manifesting in the quality of compassion. And if we elevate ourselves to develop love and compassion, we become strong in our I, no longer remaining 'weak' in our 'spirit'. Through this spiritual strength our *conscience* forms, which calls us to perform Christian deeds.

Thus let us once again absorb the mantric words of the Samaritan verse:

> *As long as you experience the pain*
> *Which leaves me unscathed*
> *Christ working in world being*
> *Is unperceived.*
> *For weak the spirit remains*
> *When alone in its own body*
> *It stays immune from feeling suffering.*

We can see from this verse that Christ is *always* at work in all being. Yet it is up to us whether He is also perceived. This depends on whether we can awaken compassion, love and conscience in ourselves, as qualities of Christ. These three qualities are expressions of the sense of I; for in authentic love our own needs are not what counts, but rather our capacity to sacrifice ourselves for the good of another. And compassion too is the full encompassing of our 'neighbour's' destiny and circumstances. The crowning virtue of the I sense, however, is conscience, which lives in us when we are not immured, alone, in our 'own body' but experience the other's spirit and act accordingly. This conscience can today lead to perception of the working of Christ in 'all being', and eventually to our own deed of sacrifice which is performed for the good of another. We thereby embark on the path of redemption of the Representative of Humanity. And this path of redemption, pursued for the sake of the other's salvation, is the medicine to heal every human being.